RUTH R
WYL

THESE HAUNTED TIMES

VOLUME ONE

To my husband – always patiently hearing the same stories over and over from me as he accompanies me to talks and interviews! And for being brave enough to come ghost hunting with me....

PROLOGUE

People often ask me what started my interest in the paranormal.

The answer is very simple: for one part of my later childhood and up until I left home to get married, my family and I lived in a house in Oaklands, an outlying estate with properties of varying ages. The area counts as part of the village of Welwyn, even though we were a little way out of the village itself, along the old Great North Road towards Knebworth, in Hertfordshire.

We had a poltergeist in that house, and it was that which sparked my interest in paranormal and my desire to research and write about it. My mother was a highly intelligent, practical woman, who had been a Radio Engineer in the Royal Air Force at a time when there was no such thing as women in engineering – and she had to fight tooth and nail to be allowed on the courses and to get her qualifications.

She was not given to flights of fancy, and so when weird things happened in our house she would try to find the logical, rational explanation. I think this pragmatic attitude was partly what instilled in me the need to look into these events more deeply.

We had also sorts of strange events in that house – some of which I have written about in the prologues to my other books. Some were of the strange noises, or lights flicking themselves on and off variety, and others were much more visceral: like the way something would pound violently on the bathroom door when my poor sister would try and take a bath. Other times, objects would be moved right in front of your eyes, in plain daylight: like the tea towel my mother and I watched fold itself neatly into a square, or the knife which started lazily spinning on the table, slid to the edge, then kept on spinning (like a sycamore seed does) for quite some distance before it eventually hit the floor.

When researching for this book, I asked on social media whether anyone had experienced anything in that street. I got some interesting replies about the nearby area (see the entry for Welwyn, Oaklands and Digswell further on), and amazingly, one lady from the same Close we lived in contacted me privately and asked me which house I was referencing. She did not live at our old house, but went and asked the current residents on my behalf. Between them, they pieced backwards through the various owners, including my own family, and worked out that they had never heard of anything "ghostly" happening there. There is certainly no activity there now. Even one of our old school friends saw my request and got in touch, laughing that me and my sister were probably pulling pranks.

It gave me pause for thought though. Our poltergeist was quite active - something weird would happen every few months, and we never knew what was causing it. Now either it ceased to happen once we moved out of the property, or people have not mentioned that things happened to them since. There is a school of thought that poltergeists are either caused by or attracted to teenage girls, and certainly my sister and I fit the category at that time. Maybe activity ceased **because** we left.

Or maybe, when you think about the fact that in piecing together the list of the various occupants, including my own family, and being certain nothing ghostly had ever happened there in that period of some fifty years backwards, those helpful neighbours were perhaps unknowingly proving a point about why researching the paranormal is so very difficult.

Our family had a lot of happenings. It caused tension sometimes, or was completely unimportant at others - but it was a fact of our lives at that house. And yet that has left no "memory" in the area about it: not with neighbours nor with our school friends.

I asked my closest friend from back then what her recollections were. She remembers me telling her about a couple of incidents when they happened – but most things she is sure I never told her about until much later in life. As she points out – had she known the full extent she would not have come round to the house! That suggests to me that we mostly "kept quiet" about it – presumably for fear of ridicule, or for fear of causing other people's fear!

The following are all accounts from people who were brave enough to come forward and tell me what happened in their lives. How many more are out there which people "keep quiet" about……

The tales I write rely heavily on you, the public, giving me your stories and talking to me about the weird things that happen. I try to recount it with as much accuracy as I can, and I try to find correlations between occurrences in locations – hoping that one day the data I collect will help definitively answer the question: *what are ghosts?*

Please don't keep quiet. Email me with your accounts –

    wa-1400@outlook.com

And if you find yourself enjoying this book, please leave a review – it really helps us authors!

Connect with me on social media as Ruth Roper Wylde

Other books by me:

    The Ghosts of Marston Vale
    The Almanac of British Ghosts
    The Roadmap of British Ghosts

Happy ghost hunting!

    Ruth Roper Wylde
    22.11.2019

THESE HAUNTED TIMES – VOLUME ONE

AMPTHILL, Bedfordshire – RECTORY LANE

A lady wrote to me to tell me about the time she spent living in a property in Rectory Lane in Ampthill, between 1969 and 1976. Ampthill is a compact little market town in central Bedfordshire, with a very small and picturesque market square which celebrated 800 years of holding a licence for a Thursday market in 2019.

Our witness bought the house in 1969 with her then husband, and the couple moved in with their three month old son. At the time they moved in, the property was part way through a conversion aimed at turning what was the original hayloft into a living space. At that time, there was an open plan staircase leading up to the hayloft space, and the old wooden hay bale doors were still present. The family were therefore still occupying only the ground floor space, which was one large open plan room and three smaller rooms, one of which was chosen to be the baby's bedroom.

One autumn evening not long after they moved in, our witness was sitting by a cosy fire with her back to the wooden staircase, and facing the small window. Her husband was sitting to her right and the two were quietly relaxing.

Suddenly, she was aware of a strange, cold feeling behind her and turned to see an indistinct foggy shape drift down the wooden stairs and out through the small window. Her husband, who was reading at the time, glanced up and exclaimed, "What was that?"

Puzzled, they made enquiries locally the next day as to what it could have been, and were told that when the property was still the stables to the main house, a young stable lad had fallen in love with one of the occupants of the main house. Of course she was far too above his social station for anything good to come of it, and with the misplaced desperation of youth at unrequited love, he hung himself from the rafters in the hayloft.

That autumnal night marked the beginning of the paranormal activity for them, as over the next few years they were frequently disturbed by the sounds of footsteps in the hayloft, and the unaccounted for sound of gunshots from the same space. I can't help but speculate whether the legend was wrong - and the lovelorn stable boy shot himself rather than hanged himself.

On one occasion, our witness heard a strange sound from the baby's room, and went in to find that a picture had inexplicably fallen from the wall where it was hanging, and was completely covering her young son's cot where he was sleeping.

This in itself made her feel uncomfortable, but had it not been for the other occurrences she would probably just have dismissed it as a fluke that the picture fell from the wall. However, by this time her son was starting to grow and toddle, and one day he suddenly fell down the stairs - and although his mother fortuitously managed to catch him before any real harm was done, he was very distressed, saying to her over and over that "the man" had pushed him.

She mentioned this to the lady that they had bought the property from, with whom she had remained fast friends. Her friend was a bit puzzled by this, because she said that her own young son had also fallen down the stairs there and kept saying his older brother had pushed him, even though that was not the case.

Over the years the family lived there, they continued to hear the footsteps and gunshots, and the sounds were heard by other family members and babysitters as well. Our witness' own mother would complain that she could not sleep at all when she stayed over due to the disturbances.

AMPTHILL, Bedfordshire - a detached house

The same witness went on to tell me about her experience in a second property she moved into some years later, still within the small sleepy town of Ampthill. By 2003, her first relationship had broken down, and she had remarried. Her new family circumstances necessitated the need for a larger family home, so when a nicely proportioned detached home came on to the market, she immediately went along to view it.

She explained, "I was greeted by the Estate Agent and I knew on stepping into the front door that the house was to be mine and not only that, I sensed something else. Saying nothing about it, I went around with the Agent. I viewed the whole house and garden and then asked the Agent for a second look at the bedroom layout to make sure we had enough room for all the family -- I also wanted to check out one particular area."

She explained to the Estate Agent that she had sensed the presence of a person from the past and asked her whether she knew if the house was haunted? Horrified, the Agent hesitated and then hesitantly explained that yes, it was, but the Vendor didn't want anybody to know in case it put prospective buyers off. Our witness assured the Agent that there was absolutely no problem as the presence felt very gentle and benign and certainly would not put her off from making an offer.

Our witness asked the Vendor about the haunting, and she was told that the young son of the family slept in the end bedroom, where, he said, a kind lady would come and sing and read to him to help him go to sleep. Apparently as well, bits of jewellery frequently and mysteriously disappeared, eventually to be found somewhere else around the house. Later, our witness asked a medium about the ghost, and was told that it was the spirit of a young lady who had died in the house many years ago whilst giving birth, and hence the fact she was attracted to young children.

Our witness went ahead and bought the house, and the family moved in whilst her husband, who worked in the Royal Navy, was working away for a few weeks. On the first few days of the move, she was unpacking and starting to set out ornaments and bits and pieces for the bedrooms, only to find to her puzzlement that they were later appearing in different bedrooms and only seemed to be left alone and undisturbed when they seemed to be in the best place!

In due course her husband arrived home and, being meticulous with his uniform, regalia and medals, unpacked and stowed everything neatly away in their bedroom chest of drawers and cupboards.

Later, once his shore leave was ended and he needed to return to duty, he went to gather his meticulously folded and stored regalia - only to find them missing. After hunting high and low, the couple eventually found them all tangled and muddled up in one small drawer.

Things settled down and family routine took over, whilst the lady of the house gradually restored the property and painted all the rooms. It took six months to complete the task to her satisfaction, and the family were all happy and comfortable living there. Her son, by now a young man in his early twenties, slept peacefully in the back bedroom until eventually moving out to buy his own house.

Occasionally the odd thing would be slightly rearranged, but for the most part nothing much happened - until her eldest stepson came to stay with his three month old baby daughter. He, his wife, and daughter were installed in the back bedroom, since the baby was not yet settling well at night and they wanted her to be in the same room as them while they tried to persuade her to sleep.

On the first night of the visit, they put the baby into her crib, and the grownups retired downstairs taking a baby monitor with them. They ate supper together as a family and chatted about their lives, and after a while realised that actually, the baby was making very little noise. Her young father said he would go upstairs and check on her - but as he rose from his chair they distinctly heard on the monitor the sound of the bedroom door quietly clicking shut, even though they had left it slightly ajar when they came downstairs.

The young father dashed upstairs to check on his daughter, but on opening the now firmly closed bedroom door found the baby girl peacefully sleeping. Surprised that she had settled so easily, and being careful not to disturb her, he tiptoed back downstairs, only to hear the sound of the door clicking open and closed again and the soft sound of someone gently humming and crooning to the baby.

There was very little activity in the house after the incident with the baby granddaughter, although one last curious incident happened when the family's Great Aunt came to stay. She was wearing some attractive rings and necklaces when she came to visit, but when she was packing to leave at the end of her stay, there was one particular ring she could not find anywhere. They searched high and low around the whole house to no avail, and eventually had to give it up as lost.

A few months later, our witness had a phone call from the Great Aunt to say that she had been clearing out some old handbags from a cupboard at home and had found the missing ring tucked into the inner purse of one of them!

AMPTHILL, Bedfordshire – CHURCH STREET

Another lady wrote to me to tell me how at one point in time, she was working for a Property Letting Agency, and there was one particular property on Church Street that was on their books as a rental property.

The house had a high turnover of tenants, because they would complain that it was haunted. There used to be a passageway between this property and the one adjoining, which had long since been sealed off and converted into a cupboard.

The tenants would complain that they could hear the sound of someone running along this passageway, even though it was now blocked off, and the noise would disturb them so frequently that they would give up the tenancy and leave. One tenant even complained that her daughter had awakened to find the ghost of a man sitting on her bed.

On one particular occasion, my correspondent and one of her colleagues were in the property performing the final inspection after a tenant had just left, when they both saw a light in one of the rooms switch itself on and then back off again. As they moved around the house, they also heard the sounds of the kitchen cupboards being opened and banged closed, even though they knew they were alone in the property. She said that the whole time they were there, the property was infused with a strange, tense atmosphere.

She also explained that there is another property further along the same street which was once an undertakers, and several people there have reported seeing a figure dressed in black, as well as some poltergeist type activity.

AMPTHILL, Bedfordshire – THE OLD POST OFFICE

And finally, for this haunted little market town, I was told that the cottage next to the Masonic Hall which is known as The Old Post Office used to have a family with two young children living there. The son was apparently frequently disturbed by what he said was another child throwing his toys about. A local medium told them it was the ghost of a child who runs through all of the houses along Church Street backwards and forwards from the White Hart pub.

ASHLEY, Shropshire – SOVEREIGN LANE

I was contacted by a witness who told me that he used to have a friend who lived on Sovereign Lane in Ashley. The property itself was steeped in history, and he was told that it was actually built over the site of a burial ground for victims of the Black Death (a plague which caused millions of deaths across Europe and peaked in the years 1347 CE to 1351 CE). There was also a nearby battle ground, that of the Battle of Blore Heath during the War of the Roses, on 23rd September 1459.

Whilst visiting his friend's house my correspondent had witnessed the bathroom taps turn themselves on and off, and the blinds on the bathroom window moved up and down of their own accord. Two antique guns affixed as decorations on the lounge wall also detached themselves and fell to the ground in a way he could only describe as "floating" – it gave him goosebumps just to recall it.

One lady told me that she had lived on Sovereign Lane for over twenty years and had never heard of any of the properties down there being haunted.

ASHLEY, Shropshire – The LOGGERHEADS PUB

Whilst trying to find out about the ghost on Sovereign Lane, I was told that nearby pub The Loggerheads is also haunted. It was originally an old coaching inn but has been much extended over its many years.

One person told me that they had a friend who used to work in the kitchens there – and had seen pots and pans move of their own accord. Apparently, they were told that there are three resident ghosts: a lady working in the kitchen, a man who appears in the garden, and a phantom dog that runs around inside the building.

On one occasion, a member of staff saw a shadow figure in the bar which seemed to walk through a patch of wall.

Another source confirmed that she and her staff had felt a presence when working in the pub both on the stairs and down in the cellars, whilst one other person told me she had once worked there for four years and had a lot of strange experiences.

It's possible that the haunting has now gone quiet, since a current resident of the pub told me that whilst interested in the stories, she had never experienced anything odd there.

One lady told me that she had heard that there was a ghost who would walk along the road from the pub down the B5026 towards Croxton. She did not recall many details about what she had been told, except that the ghost is said to be wearing a cloak, and so she wonders if it might be associated with the Battle of Blore Heath which was nearby. This was certainly a very bloody battle, with around 3,000 men losing their lives, and it ended in a rout, with the victorious Yorkists chasing the remnants of the Lancastrian forces for many miles across the local countryside.

And finally, whilst still in Ashley, one lady wrote to me to say that as a child she used to play in the churchyard there with her friends until they were told off and chased out of the grounds by the caretaker. When they described him to their parents, they were told this was actually the *former* caretaker, who had died some years previously. They never played there again.

AYR, Scotland – PARK CIRCUS

One correspondent told me about the experiences of her brother and his family.

"My brother and his wife moved into a converted Georgian house in Ayr with their two young daughters around 2000. They lived there for around fifteen years, but moved out when the marriage sadly ended. During the time they were there, there were regular bouts of paranormal activity, but with brief interludes of time where nothing would happen and the house would be quieter in a spiritual sense."

She explained that once the family moved in, the first thing which began to occur was that the fire alarm would start to sound whenever the family entered the house. Repeated checks on its workings could never find anything wrong with it.

Her sister in law always felt the house had a "presence" within it, right from the first day they moved in, but her first real experience came a few months later one day when she came home from work. None of the other family members were yet home, so the property was empty when she walked in. Fed up with the inexplicable fire alarm antics, she "addressed" the presence she felt there, telling it that she was happy to share her home with it but to please stop trying to frighten the family. The fire alarm never "malfunctioned" again.

Sometime later, my correspondent's children and their cousins were playing in the bedroom, when a piece of wood from the sash window suddenly broke free and fell into the middle of the group of children playing on the floor. The odd thing was, it didn't come at them from the direction of the window, as one might expect if it had somehow broken free and blown in, but was dropped on them from above. Its trajectory suggested that it had broken free, floated across the room, and then dropped when it was over the top of them.

On another occasion, her niece suffered an instance of sleepwalking, and was found standing in the dining room facing the mirror and repeating into it over and over again "I want my life back". Although her parents led her back to bed, her mother admitted to feeling very spooked by the incident and the strange words.

During the whole time the family lived there, the three daughters refused to be alone in the building at any time. My correspondent said she always felt uncomfortable when she went to the top floor where the bathroom was and where the bedrooms were. This was particularly the case in the little box room that the youngest daughter used. This child would not sleep without a night light from a very young age and frequently complained that she heard voices outside her room. This was corroborated by her cousin, who said when she stayed over she could hear men's voices whispering at night on the upstairs landing area outside the bedrooms.

One of the most disturbing events happened to my correspondent's sister in law one night when she was in bed, with the light on. Her husband, the brother, was downstairs still. She suddenly caught sight of something out of the corner of her eye as she sat in bed, and on turning to look fully was horrified to see a man in her room.

Her first rational thought was that it must be an intruder - and she kept silent because she thought if she cried out and her husband came up unawares, he might get attacked by the man she could now see seemed to be wearing a red coloured smoking type jacket. He was holding his chest, and started to walk towards the door. She turned to watch him go, and saw him collapse to the floor. By now the unreality of what she was seeing was starting to dawn her, and she sat there for a long moment before plucking up the courage to peer over the end of the bed to where he had fallen.

There was nothing there.

Not long after that incident, in around 2003, my correspondent and family were visiting and as they all congregated on the landing to say their goodbyes at the end of their stay, her four year old son just blurted out of the blue in his sweet little innocent voice "you got ghosts here" to his uncle.

As my witness described, "By this time, other things must have been happening and we didn't discuss events anymore. My brother caught my eye and shook his head, meaning, let's not talk about it."

Much later, not long before they left the house, the brother and his family went out to a pub which was holding a quiz night, just around the corner from their home. Whilst out, the sister-in-law realised she had left her purse at home, and returned to the house to quickly collect it.

She said that as soon as she walked into the house it felt menacing, and the feeling intensified as she walked towards the stairs. Every step nearer the stairs made her more and more scared. She said the atmosphere was so thick, and somehow "busy", that she actually felt like she was in danger. She couldn't muster up enough courage to go up the stairs and she said she felt "they" wanted to kill her. She fled from the house and at first it genuinely felt as though she was being chased by a crowd of people. She was terrified, but her panicked flight took her past the church not quite opposite their house: and here the feeling of being chased left her abruptly and she immediately felt calmer and peaceful.

When I asked around locally whether anyone else knew of a haunting in the street, one local witness came forward to tell me that some 35 years ago one of the houses at one end of the road lay empty for a while and was known as the haunted house. I wonder if there was any connection.

BALDOCK, Hertfordshire – PEMBROKE ROAD

I spoke with a witness "Jake" (not his real name) who told me several stories of his encounters with the supernatural which appear in this book.

When Jake and his partner got married, they moved into a house in Pembroke Road in Baldock. They were attracted to the town because of its quaint, peaceful, slightly quirky atmosphere with buildings from numerous eras and a charming High Street filled with eclectic shops rather than the usual high street fare. The house they chose to buy was a semidetached Victorian era house, which Jake felt was very welcoming with a pleasant atmosphere right from the day they moved in.

They made friends with quite a few of their neighbours, and one day, when chatting after a talk at the Baldock festival by a local author on the supernatural, Damien O'Dell, one of the neighbours pointed out that the story in one of Damien's books actually pertained to their house! Apparently, a previous set of occupants from the mid-1980s onwards had encountered some issues in the house. A pair of trousers left on the sofa had been seen to fold themselves, a teddy bear was knocked over by an unseen hand, and footsteps were often heard when no-one was there.

Jake says they have never experienced any activity like this, but there was one occasion when his partner came home from work, and walked down their side alley to the door they usually used to enter the property, and in doing so thought they saw their brother, who happened to be visiting at the time, pottering about in the kitchen. The distance between the view through the window to actually stepping through the doorway into the kitchen is only a matter of two or three footsteps: yet on turning the corner they were astonished to find that there was no sign of anyone in the kitchen at all!

The brother, it turned out, was actually sitting in the lounge with the door firmly closed: something he could not in any way have achieved in the space of time afforded by the time it took to take just three quick steps between the kitchen window and the kitchen doorway..

On another occasion, Jake was sitting on the sofa in the lounge. The lounge was at the very front of the property, and like many Victorian houses, actually had a street door opening directly from it. Jake's sofa was placed in front of this door, preventing it from being used – in order to create a bit more space in the otherwise quite compact room. From where he sat, he had the door into the dining room in the periphery of his vision – and would every now and then think he saw movement in the dining room out of the corner of his eye, even though he knew he was alone at home that day.

Suddenly, there was a slight "ping" noise, and Jake found himself hit by a 20p coin which appeared to have been thrown at him by an unseen hand.

On other occasions, there would be "cold spots" which seemed to walk through the bathroom, and one day there was a loud bang on the window which startled Jake as he was in there at the time. He assumed at first that a bird must have hit the window as they sometimes do, as a massive crack had appeared right across the pane.

Closer inspection, however, revealed that the crack was actually on the *inside* pane of the double glazed unit. This suggests that it was possible something hit the glass from inside the room. Jake pointed out that it was also possible that the glass cracked because of a temperature fluctuation or some such other natural causes, but he hadn't noticed that it was a day when there was a particularly great differential between the temperature inside or outside, nor did he notice any other mundane possible causes.

Jake did ask the previous owner of the house whether they had ever experienced anything there, and was told that the daughter of the household had reported seeing a dark figure standing at the top of the basement steps – which would put it about 2m away from where the figure in the kitchen had been seen by Jake's partner. Two visitors to the house, independently of one another, have also reported sensing the spirit of a boy in the house.

Jake contacted me a second time a few months later, to tell me that there had been another occurrence. He had decided to try and take an "arty" photograph of his beloved older car parked outside their house earlier that evening. It was already dark outside, and he wanted to capture a shot of the car framed by the leaves of their front hedge with lighting on it to pick the car out in the darkness. To achieve this, he switched on their bright outside light. He was using the sophisticated camera on his Iphone, and took the first shot using the camera's built in flash mechanism.

The resulting picture had too much light in it and didn't achieve the effect he was looking for, so he turned the camera's flash mechanism off, and took another shot, knowing the camera was capable of using the ambient light from their outside light to provide enough illumination.

However, just as he took the shot, the outside light turned itself off: resulting in a photograph with virtually no light on the car. Frustrated, he took a photo of the light switch and sent it to me to show how it had been thrown from the on position into the off position in that split second.

Jake says that having become friendly with their neighbours in the street, they found that other properties also have supernatural visitors. One couple reported that on several occasions they found their kitchen taps turned fully on, and once they even came downstairs in the morning to find all of the dining chairs had been placed on the top of the table: very much like the famous scene from the film "Poltergeist".

Another neighbour has reported seeing a Roman soldier in their garden – and certainly it is a matter of record that there have been nearly two thousand Roman era burials discovered within the town limits of Baldock.

Jake was also told that on nearby Jackson Street, one of the houses was apparently plagued for a few years by knocking noises which could neither be pinned down nor stopped. Eventually, during some renovation work on the heating system, a skeleton was found under the hallway floorboards! As is routine in such matters, the police were involved until it was determined that the bones dated to the end of the 19th Century. The knocking noise stopped after that: but it is always possible that might have been attributable to the newer heating system and pipes.

There is also another property nearby where someone glanced out of their window – to see a group of silent people standing in her garden for a brief moment….

BALDOCK, Hertfordshire – VARIOUS

Other witnesses from Baldock also came forward to talk about a haunted house not far from the station. It seems there is a house which spent some time partially derelict and which was thought of as haunted. The house is set at a slightly odd angle to the current road layout, suggesting that it actually follows an older alignment. It fronts onto Ickneild way but backs onto the Royston Road, and it actually got a mention in my last book "The Roadmap of British Ghosts". People would spend time there when teenagers hanging out at "the haunted house" hoping something would happen – or hurry quickly past it hoping nothing would!

One witness recalled hearing a story that there was a ghost of a young girl there, who had committed suicide by hanging herself from the branches of an old oak tree, and who would sometimes walk out in front of passing cars before disappearing.

One lady remembered venturing up the stairs inside and taking home with her a piece of broken mirror as a souvenir. The same day, her Mum's handbag was stolen, and the worried teenager superstitiously returned the broken fragment the next day in case it was bringing bad luck with it.

One property on Church Street used to be a pub called The Eight Bells, and the current resident was told that it houses the ghost of a former landlady who died in around 1604 or so. However, the earliest record of the building as a pub that I could find was from 1727, but that doesn't mean it wasn't in use earlier – just that records were not kept as well.

The witness said that they had heard their piano suddenly and randomly play two notes, and on another occasion heard footsteps coming up from the cellar – which sounded so real that she called out, thinking it was her son. She and her husband were in the same room together and both heard the steps – then realised that actually, no-one else was home...

BARGOED, Wales – GLADSTONE VILLA

I was kindly given permission to use this story by Andrew, and you can see him talking about his experiences in a video on YouTube if you are interested – simply look for "The Ghost of Gladstone Villa".

Andrew grew up in Gladstone Villa in the small mining town of Bargoed in South Wales, from his birth in 1969 until the family moved out in 1978 when he was nine years old. His grandparents lived there along with his newly married parents, so there were three generations of the family living together in the grand old property. It was a pale coloured, three storied, Victorian era house, with a twin-gabled front, on the Cardiff Road within the town itself.

Andrew recalls that the first thing the family remembered happening, not too long after he was born, was hearing a strange noise from up in the attic, as if someone was moving things about and had then opened the hatch and jumped down onto the landing. When the adults went to investigate, they found the loft hatch mysteriously open. They also heard inexplicable tapping sounds.

Whatever had been up there, seemed then to have moved downstairs and taken up residence in his grandparents' bedroom. One day, when his sleeping cot was in there, his parents found his pillow torn into two halves, and they were alarmed enough by this to take the baby and cot out of that room and settle him somewhere less active.

Most evenings, as the family sat in the lounge which was below the grandparents' bedroom, they could distinctly hear footsteps walking the room above their heads. Andrew's grandfather would often turn the television down and track the movements of whatever it was by pointing at the ceiling and commenting in his strong Welsh accent, "he's by here now!"

One day, Andrew's mother went upstairs to get his father up for work so he could get ready for his night shift. When she entered their bedroom, she was confronted by the sight of the ironing board placed on her husband's torso as he slept. When she woke him, he was astonished to find the situation he was in. He suspected his own father Bill was playing pranks, but over time, as more things began to happen around the house, he realised that was not the case.

I also spoke to Andrew's mother, who told me that many times they would hear bangs on the ceiling in the lounge, but nothing could ever be found, and she also remembered how the long electricity cord for the television would sometimes bounce up and down on the floor as if someone were tugging hard on it.

One evening, Andrew recollects lying on his bed facing the window, with his light on, when he felt something jump up on the bed behind him. When he turned to see what it was, there was nothing there – but there were claw marks on the bed and he believes it may well have been the ghost of their old Labrador dog "Tovy" who had passed away some time before.

Sometimes the family would hear the sound of a baby crying when there was no baby in the house, and on other occasions there would be loud bangs which they could find no explanation for. Sometimes, when the grandfather, Bill, tried to play his records on a Sunday afternoon as the family gathered for their Sunday dinner, the record player would keep turning itself off.

A friend suggested that they get a medium in to investigate the property, which the parents agreed would be a good idea. They contacted a medium, who came out and walked around the house. When he tried knocking on the ceiling, there was the distinct sound of something knocking back! The medium was not able to determine who or what the ghost was, so the family decided to get a priest out and have the house blessed.

The priest came and blessed the property and after a few prayers, he duly left and this seemed to have a positive effect, for a while at least, and the activity died down. Then one evening, Andrew's mother came into the house and saw the figure of a man standing by the lounge doorway. She described him as wearing what looked like a monk's habit, with the hood pulled up in such a way as to obscure his face from view. When I spoke with her, she described him as a priest. She also remembered how the lights would turn themselves on and off.

From that sighting onwards, the activity again seemed to gather pace. Sometimes they would hear what sounded like Gregorian chanting coming from the bathroom, and things would knock or bang with no explanation. The family took to sleeping downstairs with the lights on, and began to refer to the entity as "Johnny". Although the grandfather did sometimes try sleeping upstairs, he gave it up after he awoke on one occasion completely unable to move, and was sure he had heard something in the room with him.

Andrew's mother remembered going upstairs one day and walking into one of the bedrooms to be greeted by the spine chilling sight of a milk bottle floating in mid air. She told me that she hated living there as there was no respite - things would happen day or night - and she wished to never have to experience anything like it again.

One family friend in particular used to visit most evenings -and would habitually sit in the chair by the fire, chatting and watching T.V. One evening as he sat there, with Andrew playing quietly with his toys on the floor, there was an almighty bang from upstairs - so loud that the friend visibly ducked his head expecting something to come down around his ears. Although the family checked, there was nothing they could find to account for the sound.

Andrew's grandmother also had her own experiences. One day she went upstairs by herself and saw the boiler cupboard door slowly swing wide open wide by itself. She didn't stay there to see what was causing it, but rushed out and away downstairs. On another occasion she said she had the sensation of material pulling out from under her foot, as if she had inadvertently stepped on someone's floor-length gown. It was she who gave the ghost the pet name "Johnny".

Andrew also recalled an occasion when his mother had an operation on her foot and had to get around on crutches. A nurse would visit her at home to dress the wound and make sure it was healing well, and when she came to the house on one such occasion, she knelt at her charge's feet. As she knelt there tending to the bandaging she asked Andrew's mother to stop holding on to her - but both his mother and grandmother were present and could see no-one living was actually touching the nurse. They didn't dare contradict her for fear of frightening her.

Andrew did research the house in later years, and discovered that a baby called Elvin had died in the house in 1924, which might well account for the sound of a crying baby that was sometimes heard.

Eventually, the family decided to move out, and the property was sold on. The frontage was remodelled to create extra space, but after a few years the building fell into disuse, and the whole lower floor was boarded up to prevent vandalism. It still looks like that today.

I also spoke to one of Andrew's childhood friends, who remembers visiting the property to play with Andrew as a very young child - from the age of around four years old. This would have been in the early 1970's and her grandmother was very friendly with Andrew's, so the two children would be left to play while the grown-ups spent time together. She would go there on quite a regular basis throughout her childhood, right up until the family left the property.

She particularly remembers an occasion, at the age of about six years old or so, when they were playing up in the attic together. She told me that she was quite a tomboy as a child, so liked to play with the same toys as Andrew. In the corner of the attic, there was an old fashioned full sized child's rocking horse. The two children were happily playing with other toys and were neither near the rocking horse nor had they been playing with it. She specifically remembers it suddenly starting to rock - and getting faster and faster before suddenly stopping its motion dead. She doesn't remember being particularly scared - they were too young to think about ghosts or such things so just brushed it off as something odd and carried on playing.

She also explained that whenever she walked down the stairs at the property, she would feel as if someone was just behind her. She would often sidle down the stairs with her back to the wall, just because she felt like there was someone there. The only other time in her life she has experienced anything similar was at another house in Bargoed, where she would sometimes get a hard poke in the shoulder as she walked down the stairs.

She also remembered hearing banging on regular occasions from elsewhere in the house when there were only four of them in the house.

She remembers the adults would sometimes talk about the house, and the strange things that would happen there like things moving from one room to another. Her own grandmother used to read tea leaves and had quite a strong belief in the supernatural - but she would often say that you had more cause to be afraid of the living than the dead. She instilled in her granddaughter the thought that the paranormal was nothing to be afraid of, as spirits were only trying to communicate and would not cause harm. She has a vague recollection that at some time she heard that there was an old tunnel between Gladstone Villa and the Raffa club opposite - but she is not sure whether that has ever been verified.

Another correspondent told me that his family owned the property before Andrew's did, and that his father used to tell the tale of how they once heard a rhythmic tapping on the front door in the middle of the night. When they went down to investigate and opened the door, a horse was standing there and pushed its head in through the open door!

His father said the place was very creepy to live in, as you always had the feeling that someone was watching you. His grandfather was also scared stiff of the property and hated going there.

My correspondent had also been told that there were once tunnels leading from the house to the farm opposite, which once stood where today the Raffa Club stands. There was also supposed to be another tunnel leading to Gelligaer church which was used as a monk's bolt hole, from a time in history when to be a catholic monk was to be persecuted mercilessly. As the crow flies, the church is about two miles away, so that's not entirely unfeasible, if a little unlikely.

Another of Andrew's friends told me that he could not recall much in the way of actual detail now, since it was all so long ago, but he remembers being profoundly scared when he was at the property.

The Raffa club, which still stands, is also said to be haunted by a monk-like figure, and several locals remembered that it had this reputation when I asked, with rumours of disembodied footsteps and an entity who would push people working there.

BARNET, Outer London – KING GEORGES FIELD

One lady told me that sometime around 2015 or 2016, whilst walking in King Georges Field in Barnet, she and a friend had a very strange experience. They were walking along in the second field from the top, walking up hill.

They were amiably chatting as they walked, when suddenly ahead of them they noticed a bright white light. It was momentarily stationary against the hedge behind it. As they stopped to stare at it, the light seemed to hesitate a second, and then "ran" (her word) towards them – passing in between the two astonished friends.

She described it as more or less humanoid in shape – with two arms and two legs – and that there was no sense of aggression or attack in its movement. She and her friend "just stood there gobsmacked and then started laughing from excitement".

She has often thought that it felt to her like it was a very old spirit showing a moment from the past, and wonders whether it was a spirit connected with the Battle of Barnet.

BARNET, Outer London – Hadley Woods

A witness told me about an experience which she described as "horrible" in Hadley Woods.

She was walking along, when something suddenly shouted right in her ear, and at the same time blew her hair up and around, so that it fell across her face in disarray. She wasn't able to work out what it had shouted - but it was definitely a human voice even though she was alone.

Another person told me that they had heard the woods were haunted by a headless rider on a horse, whilst a third told me that they knew of someone who had performed an exorcism in the woods to cleanse the spirit.

BARNET, Outer London - JACKS LAKE

A correspondent told me about an unnerving experience he had when he was about fifteen years old - around 45 years ago. This would have put it sometime in the mid-1970s.

He was spending a happy weekend indulging in his favourite hobby of overnight fishing, and was peacefully watching his rod and line just as the sun rose over the pretty lake he had chosen for his adventure. It was a still, bright morning, with a heavy mist hanging over the water catching the early morning sunlight. As he sat there, another fisherman came wandering up to him, and asked him whether he knew the woman who had been standing on the other side of the lake staring at him for some time.

Surprised, as he wasn't expecting anyone to come and watch him fish, he peered through the mist in the direction the fisherman pointed. He could clearly see, standing there in the mist, a lady wearing what looked like some sort of floor length cape. (In the 1970's, this would not be quite as odd as it might seem with today's fashions).

Curious as to who she was and why she was staring at him like that, he decided to take a walk around the shore of the lake in order to speak to her to find out what she wanted.

As he strolled around the lake he was watching her, making sure that he didn't lose sight of her as he walked. To his astonishment, as he drew nearer, she just faded slowly out of view even as he watched. There was no question of her having moved away – it was an open area with nothing to obscure his view, but moreover, he actually saw her fade out of existence.

Not surprisingly, he felt too spooked to carry on fishing, returned to his camping spot, hurriedly packed up his belongings, and beat a hasty retreat back to the safety of home.

Two other witnesses came forward to say that they had also heard there was a ghost at the lake.

BARNET, Outer London – OAKHILL PARK

In 1985, according to one source, a couple called Jill and Malcolm were walking through the park after midnight, when they encountered a black form floating a little way above the ground. They thought they were seeing the slow moving shape of a headless human form, and became particularly alarmed when it seemed to turn towards them. They very quickly left – running in panic out of the park.

The same source describes another encounter in the same park, but much earlier, in the 1950s. On this occasion, a lady called Valerie was walking through the park in the early evening, on their way to meet up with other friends. Although early, it was the time of year when the sun had already set and night was falling.

They saw a gentleman sitting on one of the park benches, wearing old fashioned clothes from an earlier era, and a hat. Their path was taking them towards him, and they could clearly see him as he was illuminated by one of the lights near the bench. They were actually looking at him when he simply vanished – scaring Valerie's friend so badly that she collapsed screaming to the ground.

The same figure apparently appeared in the background of a photo taken in the 1970s, even though the photographer was certain no-one living had been in sight at the time.

One lady told me that when she was about five or six years old, she had seen a ghostly rider on a horse in the park, and had told her Nan about what she had seen. Her Nan had assured her it was probably just someone dressing up. However, a few years later she heard at school one day that there is meant to be a ghostly rider in the park, and realised that actually - she had seen it.

Another lady told me that her parents also had an encounter with the ghostly horse and rider, around 70 years ago - sometime in the early 1940s.

Several people told me that they spent a lot of time either as children or adults in the park, and some said they made a pastime whilst children of watching and waiting for the ghost when the mist crawled down over the hill slowly obscuring everything - but never encountered anything supernatural.

Then a lady wrote to me with her own encounter: and it seems she may well be the lady mentioned by the first source I found.. She explained, "When my husband and I were teenagers aged about 17 or 18 (in about 1980) we were walking through Oakhill Park very late one evening, it was probably approaching midnight. We were on the pathway that runs adjacent to the brook. We were walking towards the pavilion (just past where the old playground used to be). It wasn't a particularly foggy night and it was probably late summer.

"A figure was coming towards us along the path. We both saw it and didn't say anything at first, then my husband said "can you see that?" We crouched down to try and get a better look, to really focus on it. It was a figure which was about one foot off the ground. It was in the shape of a man, tall and fairly slender. It looked almost as if it was someone with flared trousers on. It had a torso but no head or neck. It was moving far faster than how its legs appeared to be moving as if it were floating, but quickly.

"The figure then started to go off across the grass to our left hand side. When it drew level with us we got very scared and ran as fast as we could towards the bridge at the pavilion. We then ran up the bank up to Church Hill Road. We do believe that had we been a few moments earlier we would have met it at the bridge. And this is where we understand that there were other sightings of this said ghost.

"We always said that if ever the local paper ran a story about the ghost that we would approach them. In 1995 the Barnet Press ran such a story and they printed an article about our story. I understand that this information was reprinted in a book about Barnet and this said ghost."

She explained that over the years they have often thought about their strange encounter, and have told people about it, but nevertheless had only *one* of them seen it, by now they would really have started to doubt what they saw. However, because they saw it together, they have remained sure of what they saw that strange night.

Yet another witness came forward and told me about the encounter her mother told her about. She explained, "I spoke to my mum and the story she had been told goes as follows. My grandfather was walking home to East Barnet village after seeing my Grandma when they were still courting, and his route took him along the side of Oakhill Park.

"It was very late at night, and he noticed a man walking towards him who seemed to be dressed quite strangely in a long dark cloak and a big hat. As they approached each other, my grandfather politely tipped his hat and spoke a cordial greeting. The stranger gave no reply nor any sign of accepting the politeness, which my grandfather thought was rather rude. As they passed one another, my grandfather turned to look back at the man with a frown, but was astonished to find there was not a soul to be seen."

Another witness wrote to me to tell the story of an encounter her father had near the park, "My Father told of a journey home from visiting my

Mum, before they were married, from New Barnet to Wood Green. This would have been sometime when they were courting between 1945 and 1949 when they married. It was very late one Christmas Eve night, and he was riding his motorcycle home along Church Hill Road beside the park, which was on his left as he rode.

"He said it was a clear crisp night with good visibility and strongly moonlight. He noticed a person walking along the edge of the park, someone wearing a type of Monks Habit with a cowl hood which was pulled over the person's head. As he neared, he slowed right down, wondering who would be out on such a cold night."

She went on to explain that as her Grandfather had passed the walker, he noticed that there were no legs or feet visible beneath the habit and so he looked up into the cowl hood - and was horrified to realise that he could not see a face - just a black shadow where features should have been. He sped off on his motorcycle - shaken to the core.

The next day when visiting his betrothed and her parents he told them all about what he had seen. Her father was very interested and commented that "You saw the ghost of Geoffrey de Mandeville, he is known to walk alongside the park".

My correspondent told me, "My Father had never heard of the reports of any of the stories about this ghost so had no preconceived ideas about what he saw. He said that he always accelerated a bit more when passing that bit of East Barnet after this."

Her father passed away in 2012 at the respectable old age of 93 having had a good life and a career as a research engineer, but he told his tale many times over the years and never wavered in the details of what he saw that night.

Another witness remembered that as a child there were always rumours to be heard of the ghostly lady being seen around the "tunnels" that took Pymmes Brook under Parkside Gardens.

Pymmes Brook runs out of the south end of Jack's Lake (see previous entry) a little further north from the park, which also has a ghostly lady, so it's possible that there is a connection.

One lady told me that tale she had heard about those tunnels. Apparently, the story went that there was once a wealthy young woman in Hadley who arranged to run away with her [presumably unsuitable] sweetheart, but instead was trapped by her angry father in a tunnel under Hadley Church where she died.

My witness was told as a child that if you listen carefully you can hear her ghost running along the tunnel crying to be let out, and remembers being scared out of her wits by the tale. Several other people came forward with tales about tunnels in the area running from the church or under the woods.

BATH, Avon – DANIEL STREET

Whilst researching for the book, I came across an account with little detail, saying that in 1987 the ghost of a man was seen in Daniel Street in Bath, in one of the mews style houses there.

I asked locally whether anyone had any experiences in the street, and a lady came forward with her own interesting story.

She explained that sometime around 2008 or so, she was visiting some friends who had a basement apartment in a house in Daniel Street. It seems likely that if there was a basement apartment, this would be in one of the old mews style houses which are often split in this way in this day and age.

As they were sitting there chatting, our witness became aware of a cold chill passing over her, which seemed to emanate from the doorway which led out onto the stairs up to the ground floor.

She glanced through the open doorway to the stairs, idly wondering what was causing the chill. To her horror she saw an old lady standing at the bottom of the stairs, holding the hand of a small child. The lady had grey hair swept back into a bun, and seemed to be weeping.

Our witness startled and gasped at the sight, just as everyone else present in the room started to comment on the sudden chill pervading the air. However, one of the group of friends started to ridicule what they were all sensing, saying it was nonsense and clearly just a cold draught of air from somewhere.

As soon as he expressed his disbelief that there was anything supernatural occurring, his chair suddenly collapsed beneath him, dumping him unceremoniously onto the floor.

My witness said that overall, the property always had a strange feeling about it, and none of the group of friends would ever go and use the toilet at the end of the corridor, because everyone felt spooked in there.

I can't help but wonder whether there is any correlation between the original entry I had found and this address.

BEDFORD, Bedfordshire – AMPTHILL ROAD

A lady, whom we shall call Katie, wrote to tell me her story. In 1995, she and her husband were living in a relatively modern semi-detached house in Ampthill Road in the county town of Bedford.

At that time, their son was a small baby, who slept in a typical child's cot with toys tied to the railings. He was normally a very calm baby, and would sleep through the night from quite an early age: and even if he did happen to wake, he was usually content to lie and quietly amuse himself with the toys within his reach.

However, one particular night he woke screaming and crying hysterically, and no amount of nappy changing, feeding, rocking or cuddling could console him – until they took him out of his room and into their own bedroom where he immediately calmed down and once again became their usual placid, easygoing son.

As the couple sat there on their own bed, quietly puzzling together over what had upset their child so badly, they both distinctly heard the bell attached to one of the toys on the side of the cot start ringing.

There were no open windows or doors to cause a breeze, and they had no other children or pets. So who was ringing the little bell?

Fortunately for their child's peaceful sleep, this was the only night this ever happened. The only other occurrences Katie could remember from their time in that house was that sometimes they would come down in the morning to find the kitchen doors standing open – when they had definitely not been left that way.

BEDFORD, Bedfordshire – Goldington Road

In 1945, the Bedfordshire Police Force under Commander Willis purchased the property known as "The Pines" at 55 Goldington Road as their new headquarters. The building was adapted for its new purpose, and started work as its new life in 1947. It remained in service until a new purpose built station was commissioned in nearby Kempston, and the force moved its headquarters there in the late 1970s.

One lady wrote in to tell me that she used to work in this old headquarters, and it was rumoured that the old Chief Constable still wandered the floors of the building he had commissioned even after his death.

She described how when they were working the night shift, they used to hear footsteps go right across the floor they were working on, from one end to the other. Considering there were actually now partition walls in between to create individual office spaces, and the area was fully carpeted, it should actually have been impossible to hear such footsteps since no living being could possibly walk through walls and make distinct footstep noises on carpeted floors.

Furthermore, they were on the night shift, and therefore locked in. Nevertheless, on one particular night it got so bad with the footsteps being so distinct, that one of the crew members called out the dog handler.

The dog handler arrived with his fully trained, brave Alsatian police dog, and was briefed as to what the problem was: that prior to starting their shift they had checked all of the rooms and locked the doors, and yet they could still hear someone walking about. The dog handler set off to perform a search of the area, and with a quiet command put his dog into working mode. His was a dog who had happily searched out and helped to bring down and arrest many a criminal, and was keen and eager to get down to business.

However, the dog made it as far as the first floor landing, where he stopped dead in his tracks, whined, and refused point blank to go any further. Nothing would persuade him to move – and the footsteps carried on unabated for another hour until nearly 4am in the morning.

BEDFORD, Bedfordshire – PILGRIMS FEED MILL, ST LEONARDS STREET.

Today, St Leonard's Street in Bedford is a quiet residential street, with older terraced cottages leading to the newer houses at the end of the cul de sac. These newer houses are built over what used to be the site of WH and J Rogers Flour Mill.

One evening in the 1970s, when the mill still existed, some young lads were playing football in the street. It was around 9pm at night, on a summer's evening, just as dusk was starting to fall, and not long before their mothers would start calling them in for bed.

As they played, one of them was a bit over enthusiastic with their kick, and the ball rolled under the closed and locked gates of the mill, which was closed up for the night and standing empty and deserted in the failing light.

The lads were arguing who was going to scramble over the gates go and get it, when one of them suddenly noticed the shadowy figure of a man standing next to one of the fork lifts. Horrifyingly, he seemed to be carrying his own head under his right arm.

Screaming, the boy pointed out the apparition, which was then seen by several of his companions before they all decided to run home and perhaps get an earlier night than originally planned.

When they asked their parents about it the next day, they were told that a worker had died there by sticking his head into the grain silo as the grain came thundering down the chute: effectively beheading him.....

One of the group of boys also lived on St Leonards Street. He recalled that occasionally they also had strange happenings in the house they lived in. Sometimes, when you stepped into the kitchen, there would be a strange mist hovering in the air, which would slowly dissipate.

On one occasion, his sister was walking out of the kitchen and into the adjoining dining room, which involved taking one step up as the floor levels were slightly different. As she took the step, a milk bottle came flying out of the kitchen behind her and smashed on the floor just behind her foot. At the same second, she stumbled forward as if someone had given her a good shove from behind.

There was no-one else in the kitchen at the time.

BENTLEY, WALSALL, West Midlands - STEPPING STONE CLOSE.

This charmingly named small urban close of pleasant semi-detached houses, surrounded on three sides by open field areas, hides at least one oddity.

A gentleman correspondent wrote to tell me about his experience living in one of the houses there, during the 1990's. There were only three people living there in the family at that time and he himself was a child, but he always felt there was something a bit weird about the house.

When they were downstairs, and none of them upstairs, they would hear the sounds of footsteps walking around the upstairs room. As soon as one of them dashed up the stairs to investigate the noise, the sound would abruptly stop.

The family cat, normally a pleasant animal, would sometimes lash out physically and hiss as if attacking something - even though the humans could perceive nothing there. On other occasions, my correspondent's toys would vanish, and couldn't be found anywhere. Then weeks later, the missing toy would suddenly turn up in a completely random and inexplicable place.

As he says, the "big moment" eventually came, and he describes it like this, "It was (ironically) during the craze over the release of the film "Ghostbusters" that I had received a replica Ghostbusters fire station toy that I kept in my bedroom. I went up to bed one night and discovered that I was unable to get into my bedroom because no matter how hard I tried the door just would not open."

Upon investigation by the adults, it was discovered that his toy fire station had moved the entire length of his bedroom, the carpet had been lifted and the station was wedged under the carpet: effectively blocking off the door and preventing entry. All three occupants of the house had been downstairs together all evening: and even if one of them had sneaked up and somehow lifted the carpet and shoved the toy under it in such a way as to wedge the door shut…. it would have left that person effectively trapped inside the room by their own prank!

BERKHAMPSTEAD, Hertfordshire – NEW ROAD

Whilst researching for my last book, The Roadmap of British Ghosts, one correspondent mentioned a particular copse of trees as being haunted, which intrigued me.

She described it as "As you go up New Road and it opens up to fields on your left hand side there is a circle of trees that are supposed to be haunted. My daughter and I still get the shivers when walking in it."

Curious, I asked around and found all sorts of local knowledge about the place. A common one that several people knew was that it was once a site which attracted devil worshippers, and some severed chicken heads had been found there. It is described as a perfect circle of trees, which is interesting in itself.

One correspondent said there was also a perfect ring of conifer trees nearby. Several people agreed that the woods all around here are "spooky" or "atmospheric", with a "dark feeling".

There is a nearby legend of a Black Shuck, known as The Black Dog of Tring, which was said to be the spirit of a murderer who was hanged in 1751. A Black Shuck was something mostly reported during medieval times, and was thought to be a harbinger of death or ill fortune. They appeared like huge dogs – the size of a calf – and were often described as having glowing red eyes.

One person also recalled that not far from this ring of trees, but along the actual road itself, there used to be sightings of a female ghost wearing early Victorian style dress.

BIGGLESWADE, Bedfordshire - HITCHIN STREET.

One lady I interviewed told me about her experience in a house on Hitchin Street in Biggleswade. She and her first husband moved into the property in 1985. It was a quaint little cottage which they were renting in a quiet residential street. It was a mid-terraced, two up two down type cottage so common across Britain - very small, but quite neat with a pebble dashed frontage.

When they moved in, she straight away began to wonder if they had done the right thing renting the place, because it had an oppressive, gloomy atmosphere about it. To try and make it feel more welcoming, the young couple immediately set about redecorating the place in bright airy colours. However, even as each room steadily became lighter and better looking with their efforts, the gloomy atmosphere persisted - and the young couple found that often when they were home, they would end up bickering and fighting with each other, whereas away from the property they would feel perfectly happy in one another's company.

Their bedroom was over the front room, facing the street. It had a built in cupboard along one wall with an old fashioned wooden door, and they placed a large sideboard along one of the other walls.

In the centre of the sideboard, there was a huge free standing mirror in a heavy frame with big chunky feet. It was heavy enough that it took two people to lift and maneuver it.

The young housewife liked to collect perfume bottles, and had quite an impressive display which she proudly arranged on her sideboard, in front of and to both sides of the huge mirror.

One night, as they lay in bed asleep, they were awakened by a strange noise, and her husband sat up in bed, moving his head from the pillow as he did so. Seconds later, the mirror crashed down across his pillow - upside down. Had he not moved, he could have been quite badly hurt.

When they inspected the damage, they found the true extent of the bizarre nature of what had just occurred. On the sideboard, you could clearly see where the bottles which had stood on either side of the mirror had been pushed aside – as if someone had needed space to get their hands on the mirror. The bottles lined up so prettily in front of the mirror were all completely undisturbed. The mirror itself had landed upside down across where his head had been.

This meant in order to get from point A to point B, the mirror had to have been lifted up and over the bottles, turned upside down, and then dropped with such force that it broke the heavy wooden frame...

My witness told me that she still has nightmares today about the built in cupboard in the room – it just had such a bad feeling emanating from it. They kept mundane things such as suitcases and Christmas decorations in there, and every time they opened it they would find the contents had been completely rearranged. Sometimes they would hear scrabbling noises from inside, and a cold feeling would often seep out into the room from it.

Eventually, the couple had called their Reverend in and asked him for help with the property. He visited, and physically shivered as soon as he entered the house. He said that he could feel that someone had died at the foot of their stairs. He thought that the original owner of the cottage was haunting it, and was unhappy that other people were living in "his" home. The Reverend warned them that they would never be able to live happily there.

They only stayed there for a total of eleven months before deciding they could not stand it anymore. They moved out as soon as they could find somewhere else to rent.

When I asked locally for any corroboration, I was told that one gentleman used to live on Hitchin Street and often heard the sound of a horse galloping down the street outside during evenings or late at night.. even though there were clearly no horses around.

BIRCHAM NEWTON AIRFIELD, Norfolk

This old airfield in Norfolk actually saw service in both World Wars, housing bomber squadrons for much of its active life. During the Second World War, the airfield was an important Coastal Command station: responsible for tasks such as mine laying, reconnaissance, anti-shipping strikes and air-sea rescue.

It was finally closed as an active RAF airfield in December 1962. There is a legend that the site is haunted by the crew of a Lockheed plane which crashed there – most sources say it was a three man crew, but some say there was also a woman and that her spirit is present too.

The area of the base which is most frequently reported as being actively haunted is the former squash courts. It is claimed that many investigating crews have recorded both sound and visual phenomena here. Supposedly the sounds of a squash game in progress can be heard, and sometimes the sounds of an active airbase. Doors are said to open and close by themselves, and sometimes phantom aircraft are heard flying overhead.

One correspondent wrote to me to say that he had worked at the site for over 40 years before retiring a year or so ago, and at one time he possessed a tape recording he made when one of the paranormal teams were there investigating. His tape recorded the inexplicable sounds coming from the squash courts, but unfortunately, he says, in the intervening years the tape is now missing. He said that during the whole time he worked on site (mostly in the hospital wing or Study Centre B) there were always tales of things people had heard, seen, or felt.

Another gentleman wrote to me to say that he used to live close to the site around thirty years ago, and spent time around the squash courts. He stated quite firmly that he doesn't believe in ghosts at all, yet found the squash courts creepy (his word) enough to write and tell me about them all these years later. He said there would be unexplained cold spots even on very hot days, and noises they could find no origin for. He said the place always made him feel very uneasy.

Interestingly, one lady told me that another area on the site was the old hospital area - and there is a corridor which used to lead to the morgue which still has a very unsettling feeling to it.

Another lady wrote to me to say that she moved into one of the houses that is now on the edge of the old site, in around 2013 or so. Since moving in, they have had all sorts of paranormal experiences. She told me that one of the first things she remembers noticing happened not very long after they moved into their new home. She was alone in the house one evening, taking a relaxing bath, when she distinctly heard the sound of a man coughing. She told me that it sounded as if the man were sitting on the sofa in her living room.

At the time, their young daughter was only two years old, and far too short to be able to reach up to light switches. Yet on a number of occasions, when she went to check that her daughter was sleeping peacefully, she would find the bedroom light turned on, where she knew for certain it had previously been off.

On another occasion, her mother and sister came to babysit for her while she went out for the evening. When she came home, they were quite worried - and told her how at one point during the evening they had heard the child giggling. They went in to check on her and settle her back down, but found her sitting cross legged in the middle of her room on the floor. She was still fast asleep, but seemed to be talking to someone as if that person were sitting opposite her.

On another night, my witness was herself asleep in bed, when the sound of her dog frantically barking and snarling suddenly woke her up. As she woke, she saw the dark outline of a figure rushing towards her from the corner of the room. Instinctively knowing it wasn't a "real" intruder, she did what every self-respecting one of us would do, and hid under the duvet.

Her dog, also of the opinion that discretion was the better part of valour, hid under the bed. The two of them remained quivering like this for about half an hour, before she plucked up the courage to throw off the duvet, switch the light on, and run from the room accompanied by her furry protector.

It was around 3am in the morning, but she was too scared to go back into the bedroom and try to sleep, so she decided to try and occupy herself by resuming her half-finished chore of painting the bathroom.

On other occasions she has startled awake in the middle of the night to see a figure standing beside her bed before it fades away. Her boyfriend has also seen the figure - one evening he was in the kitchen when, as he told her later, he thought he saw her come in behind him and put her bag down on the kitchen side. He asked her if she wanted a cuppa, as he was about to make one, but she didn't reply. He turned around to look at her fully and repeat his question - only to find there was no-one in the kitchen with him. He searched the house calling for her - before quickly realising he was still alone and she had not yet, in fact, arrived home from work.

Several other people wrote to say they had found the area around the squash courts and the swimming pool very creepy, or spooky, but had never seen or heard anything definite. One rather tantalisingly told me she and a friend had once seen a UFO (Unidentified Flying Object) fly over the site, but declined to comment further.

Another gentleman had heard stories that a security guard working there had claimed to look up at the ceiling one night when patrolling inside one of the buildings, to find that he was suddenly looking at an open sky above him with planes flying overhead.

BOSHAM HARBOUR, Sussex.

A lady wrote to tell me of her experience on a family day out to Bosham. She explained, "My family have been to Bosham Harbour many times.

Apparently it is built on the site where King Canute supposedly tried to turn back the tide and also his daughter was originally laid to rest in Bosham Church, although her remains have since been moved to Chichester Cathedral. There are crude crosses carved into the stone arch around the main door which legend says were etched by crusaders before setting sail to the Holy lands. In all the years of going there I had never read or heard anything about pirates."

She told me that the particular day which is etched into her memory was around 11 years ago, in 2008 or so. At that time her granddaughter was about five years old and my witness, her two daughters, and the small granddaughter all went to Bosham Harbour for a day out together.

They had a pleasant time sightseeing and wandering around, and part way through the day decided to pay the lovely old church a visit. The adults were admiring the interior, when the young child suddenly exclaimed loudly 'I don't like that man!'

Puzzled, the three women looked around, noting that there was no-one else present at all except themselves. They asked the little girl what man she meant, and she pointed towards the entrance and replied, "the pirate man standing over there by the door". Shrugging it off, they decided to humour her and carried on with their day, leaving the church and heading for the harbour.

When they got there the little girl again spoke up, saying, "there is the pirate, he is in his boat over there" and pointed towards the middle of the harbour. Once again, the adults could not see anyone - neither a boat nor a person were in the middle of the water. They questioned her as to where exactly she was looking, but she just shrugged and told them he had gone now, and skipped on ahead as if nothing odd had just happened.

In the way adults do, they again just shrugged it off as an incident of childish imagination, and carried on with enjoying their day, putting the incident out of their minds.

A few days later, at home and with time on her hands, my witness thought again about what her young granddaughter had said. She was intrigued, because she had not ever thought of the harbour as having any connections with pirates, so she did an internet search on the local history.

To her astonishment she discovered a legend that Bosham Church had once been plundered by Danish pirates, who stole the deeply toned tenor bell from the church belfry. They made their escape to their boat with their loot, and set sail out of the harbour. The bereft villagers ran into their church and rang the other bells to warn of the raiders, and to their astonishment the tenor bell answered its erstwhile companions, ringing out clearly across the harbour from the fleeing boat.

As it rang, the boat carrying it mysteriously ran into trouble and sank, taking all the hapless pirates down to their deaths in the cold water, along with the bell they had plundered. The legend says the bell can sometimes still be faintly heard ringing from beneath the waves, answering its companion bells when they are rung or on stormy nights.

As my correspondent said, "Needless to say, when my granddaughter says she sees/hears or senses something that we don't, we no longer brush it aside as just her imagination!"

BOUGHTON, Northamptonshire – St John the Baptist Church ruins

Boughton is one of those old English villages which have "moved" their location slightly over the centuries. This means that what was once the site of the old medieval village and its church – of which only a few scant stone ruins and the gravestones still remain – now actually are separate from the modern day buildings and bustle and stand alone and abandoned surrounded by arable land to the east of today's village.

The earliest mention of the church on this original site is 1201, but it is quite probable that there were still earlier remains prior to that. Most interestingly, there is a natural spring well which still bubbles up beneath the wall of the chancel, and which was dedicated as a Holy Well to St John the Baptist. In 1353 the area was granted licence to hold a three day fair in honour of St John. In every likelihood, although of course no records remain, this was the site of a pre-Christian sacred spot over which the church was erected.

The remaining ruins date back to the 1300's at least, and have been derelict and crumbling for long centuries in between: one writer in the 1500s described how the churchyard was already falling to ruin and disrepair by then - so overrun by rabbits digging holes that parishioners were afraid to walk through the churchyard to attend service for fear they might break their ankle in one of the holes! By 1735 the church was described as nothing but a few ruined walls, and sometime around 1785 the spire and tower finally collapsed.

According to legend there are a number of ghost attached to the church. One is that of a beautiful red haired woman. Supposedly, she will try to entice male passers-by into giving her a kiss. If anyone is foolish enough to take up her offer, they will die exactly one month later.

There is also supposed to be the spirit of a highwayman, a lady in white, and the ghosts of children playing amongst the gravestones.

As in my habit whenever I get the chance, I decided to do a spot of ghost hunting one Sunday afternoon, and chose this location as our destination for the day.

It was in August 2016, on a hot and humid day, with large thundery showers lazily making their way across the country. The showers were brief and slow moving, so any given location was just as likely to remain dry as it was to get one of these storms pass directly overhead.

I packed a picnic, my long suffering husband, and our two bouncy Belgian Malinois dogs into the car, and off we went. I am a great believer in visiting haunted sites at any time of day or night - I don't subscribe to the view that phenomena can only be recorded in the dead of night. In my experience and in my research, it seems that "things" can happen at any time and in any weather conditions – so why not enjoy a day out and a picnic at the same time as ghost hunting? The only advantage of going at night is it is quieter with less human disturbance, and it also feels more "spooky" and therefore more exciting to people.

On this particular day, we pulled up at the site a little after noon. The sun was shining brightly, the insects were buzzing, and it was hot as all get-go. We parked the car under the shade of a large tree, and then watched as a few fat drops of rain splashed onto the windscreen and an ominous dark cloud floated overhead.

Deciding that caution would be a good idea, we waited in the car and munched on our sandwiches and crisps while the very small, and actually very light, shower passed on. We had the windows open to keep the car cool, and my husband (a sceptic but happy to humour me) was asking me what ghosts we were supposed to be looking for. I was just explaining about the various ghosts, and he was asking why so many highwaymen are supposedly headless, when the sound of children singing and laughing clearly floated through the car.

Astonished, we stopped talking and looked at each other, then laughed a bit nervously and decided we would check the perimeter for nearby farmhouses the sound could have drifted from. After we finished eating, we got out of the car, and taking the dogs did a walk around as much of the perimeter as we could get to. There are no other buildings anywhere nearby. I can't explain where that sound came from.

We entered the site through an old iron gateway, and discovered that although much of it is overgrown with brambles and stinging nettles, there is a mown pathway around the actual ruins themselves, meaning you can walk around and examine what is left of the ancient stonework. You can also clearly see still the bubbling spring of clear water coming out in its little stone basin – the site is worth a visit for that alone.

We wandered around for quite some time, taking photographs and chatting. Although the day was so hot, the churchyard was pleasant in the humid air, and we had decided to let the dogs off the lead so they could play around in the stinging nettles and brambles. Belgian Malinois are big active dogs, and they were having a whale of a time trying to sniff out rabbits and voles and jumping over the low scrub.

My husband was asking me how the more formal ghost hunts I tend to attend when I can are conducted. I was explaining how the investigators will "call out" encouragingly to the spirits as a way of trying to get them to interact, and he gamely (albeit a bit laughingly) agreed to give it a go. He stood still and called out to the young children we had heard, inviting them to come out and play with the dogs we had brought with us.

To our astonishment our youngest dog - two years old at the time, and absolutely full of rambunctious idiocy - leapt out of the bush he was at that point gamely trying his best to get under about 60 feet away from us, and sat down on the neatly mowed grass facing away from us. He leant to his side and tilted his head up, exactly as if he was leaning against a person and getting a head scratch (sitting down, he comes up to the hip/ lower waist height of most adults). He maintained this position for a good ten to fifteen seconds, before getting up and bounding happily off again - all without paying us any attention whatsoever.

I had been trying to get my camera out of its bag and turned on, but had failed - so asked my husband to "call" again. He obliged, saying the whole thing had brought goosebumps out on his arms, and even though our dog was even further away from us this time, he repeated the movement almost immediately - but on a different bit of pathway. This time I was ready and snapped literally as many photos as I could in the seconds he sat like that before running off again.

Sadly, although I later carefully scrutinised every shot, there is nothing other than my dog in any of them. Interestingly though, he is now five years old and neither he, nor my other 11 year old dog, have ever behaved like this before or since - except when interacting with a "real" person.....

BOURNEMOUTH, Dorset - WEST

CLIFF ROAD

West Cliff Road in Bournemouth has a number of large properties which have been converted into small blocks of flats.

One lady contacted me and told me her story relating to one of these properties. Her tale dated back to 1965, at which time she was courting with the young lad who was later to become her husband. He was renting out a small flat on the ground floor of this property, and she would often visit him in the evenings before returning home to her Mum's house.

One day, she went round to his flat after she finished work, a bit earlier than usual, intending to cook something for when he came in and to clean around the place a bit. The building was owned at that time by an older lady, and after she had been there a little while the landlady knocked on the door to check who was in the flat, since it was earlier than normal. Once she realised that it was just her tenant's girlfriend, she came in and had a cuppa, and the two women sat and chatted for a few minutes before each going about their own business.

As her visitor left, our witness popped through to the flat's communal kitchen to fetch the vacuum cleaner, and to her astonishment saw a man sitting at the yellow Formica table with his arms folded in front of him. Not recognising him, she asked him what he was doing there. He told her his name, but it wasn't a name she recognised, and all these years later she can't recall what it was. He told her that he was just resting for a bit, as he had just dropped a load of cognac off in his lorry, and in a minute he would need to get a move on and carry on to "Fulhams".

She collected her vacuum cleaner and got on with her chores. However, something about the encounter kept nagging at her and striking her as "odd" - as if something was not quite right and she couldn't quite put her finger on it. The next day at work she told her friend about it - who went to the reference library and discovered that on the spot where the building now stood, a roadway used to run through to Longfleet - where cognac was brought in by boat.

Some months later her young man was moving out of the flat, and something triggered her memory so that she told him about the weird encounter she had with the small man in the kitchen, saying she was quite glad he was moving out. It turned out that her fiancé had also encountered the same man inexplicably sitting in the kitchen - even though he was not resident and no one knew who he was..

BRIDGNORTH, Shropshire - EBENEZER ROW

I found an original source story that said one of the cottages on Ebenezer Row was renovated in 1985, and that seemed to provoke paranormal activity. The owner reported that on several occasions, the apparition of a small old man would pass him as he went down the staircase, and sometimes would even walk straight through him.

When I asked locally, one person came forward to say that in the late 1980's this small row of cottages was part of his early morning paper round. He said that as winter drew in and the mornings became darker, he found himself getting increasingly "freaked out" (his words) when he had to deliver there. He has never been able to put his finger on what caused the feeling - but he did recall that one of the houses used to have a monthly copy of a magazine about all things "Psychic".

Unfortunately, no-one else came forward with any knowledge of the property.

BRIGHTON, East Sussex

One lady spoke to me about her experiences when she worked in a care home in Brighton back in the late 1970's and early 1980's. The property was in West Drive, and was known as St Elizabeth's. It has long since changed hands and seems to be a private residence now, as far as she is aware.

At the time, however, it was listed as a "Residential" home for old people, but in reality it was a care home with many of the residents needing constant care and help with everyday living. Our witness at the time was a teenager, and this was her first real job. She had really wanted to get into this line of work, and had asked over and over for the business owner to give her a chance and let her learn the ropes on the job as it were. Eventually, to her delight, the owner relented and agreed to give her a try.

She picked up a few shifts a week, and was really happy to find herself working in the lovely old three story house. She thinks the building was possibly Victorian, and remembers the high ceilings and big airy windows on the main floors - with smaller windows up in the third floor attic rooms. The matron/manager lived in some of the rooms on the third floor, and there was a separate back set of stairs, which suggest it would originally have been servant's quarters.

After she had been there a few weeks, she was working on one particular Wednesday afternoon, taking over the duties from the morning shift who were just finishing. Her task that afternoon was to help with the bathing of one of the residents, and she was chatting quietly with the other member of staff and the lady they were bathing. Suddenly, the door to the room swung slowly open and out on the landing there stood a tall figure wearing a long cape and wearing a pointed hat. She described how it made her think of the kind of hat that a witch would traditionally be thought of wearing.

The figure had its right arm out, as if it had just pushed the door open, and she clearly remembers that there was a purple ring on one of its fingers. Both she and the other carer saw the figure - and stared at him in astonishment, not really understanding what they were looking at, there in a private residential nursing home and in broad daylight.

The door started to swing slowly shut, and the figure just suddenly disappeared - one moment it was there, and then suddenly it was not. They had no time to really react to what had just happened - and clearly whatever they saw was not "of this world" in the sense that it was clearly not a flesh and blood person.

Although she continued to work there for some time afterwards, she never saw the thing, as they came to think of it, again - although she says the stairs always gave off a sense of something watching you as you climbed or descended....

BARSHAM, Suffolk

One witness wrote to tell me about the experience her husband had whilst driving home one night in either January or February, in approximately 2011.

It was approximately half past eleven at night, so the roads were mostly quiet with not too much traffic. He was driving from Lowestoft to Bungay, and had almost reached Barsham, when he saw an older lady walking her dog along the side of the road. Just as he thought to himself that it was odd that she was out walking along an unlit road so late at night, she seemed to look directly at him and then stepped out in front of his car.

Panicked, he swerved violently to avoid hitting her, and screeched to a stop. Although he immediately got out of the car and looked all around, there was no sign of her anywhere.

As he later pointed out to his wife, had there been any oncoming traffic the result would have been horrendous - and he has often wondered if her appearance is the cause of any accidents along there.

BURFORD, Oxfordshire - WARWICK HOUSE

When researching for my other books, several people commented on the various ghosts they were aware of in the picturesque little town of Burford in Oxfordshire, and I thought they would be worth a mention here.

One lady said that her grandmother used to live in Warwick House, a strikingly elegant Grade II listed house in the heart of the small town. My correspondent said that her grandmother would regale them with stories of her time at the grand old house, and particularly the story of the ghost she saw there on several occasions. Apparently, at around four in the afternoon, one could often encounter the figure of a man walking from the inner courtyard, down the hall, and out through the front door.

Another lady recounted the story her father used to tell them. He lived in a cottage on Church Lane which adjoins the property which housed the shop "Mrs Bumbles". He told them how one evening they were sitting in their living room talking, when suddenly a gloved hand came through the wall next to the window seat. It had only lingered a moment before disappearing, but was seen long enough to terrify her Grandmother. A gentleman responded to that – saying his own father used to relate a very similar story, and as they were all local families it seems likely he was referring to the same event. Yet another person said they remembered this story as relating to the old grammar school tuckshop called "Husseys", and that the hand came up through the window seat, before giving a little twirl and then disappearing. A little digging around shows that Husseys Tuck shop was in fact on the same site as Mrs Bumbles shop....

Another witness joined in on the discussion, saying that their own father used to relate the same story as he was also present that day in the tuckshop. He had explained to them that the window seat where the action took place was actually situated above a cellar, so one of the lads present at the time rushed downstairs thinking someone was down there and playing a joke on them – but found the cellars completely empty of any living being.

Another person told me that when she was young, she used to work in The Crypt Tea Rooms, which had the ghost of a lady who would walk through the wall. All the girls were frightened to go up to the upstairs stock room alone, but the owner at the time used to say she had seen it and it never bothered her or did any harm.

This was corroborated by another lady who worked there as a waitress as a weekend and holiday job when she was in her late teens, between 1961 and 1963. She told me that a lot of strange things happened during the time she worked there, and gave a couple of examples. She explained, "The cafe was divided into 3 rooms one behind the other, named the front, middle and back rooms. The middle room was reportedly haunted. We had the electrician in to change the light switch several times but to no avail: you would switch it on and moments later it would be switched off and vice versa. You could click the switch up and down several times and then wherever you stopped it would click back to the opposite."

She explained that even after the electrician fitted the new switch, it made no difference – whichever way you left the light switch, on or off, when you came back a few minutes later it was the other way. She said in the end they just learned to put up with it.

She also recalled that on one occasion a visitor asked her if the premises was haunted. Surprised, she asked him what had made him ask such a question, and he told her that he was a member of a paranormal research society and could feel a presence in the room.

At that time, the family who owned the business lived in the building in the upper floors. The elderly grandfather of the family lived with them and had the uppermost room on the top floor. He told the young girls working there that he was often awoken by the sensation of something like a cold wet flannel being dragged across his face. My witness was brave enough to ask him whether this scared him, but he told her that it didn't anymore as he had become so accustomed to it.

She recalled that when she first started working at the tea rooms, there was a room on the second floor, which had been boarded up and closed off – but you could tell it was there because outside you could make out the bricked up window.

Since the business was thriving, the owners decided it would pay to open up this space as an extra dining area. Accordingly, plans were drawn up and approved and the builders were engaged to break the room open and refurbish it. On the day they were making the opening into the room, the staff gathered round, curious to see what bygone treasures might be lurking in the disused space.

As the builders broke through the bricked up doorway, several of them were clustered round trying to peer into the gloom – and they all distinctly saw a figure cross the room towards them.

Once it was in use, none of the waitresses liked to service this second floor room, because even on the warmest summer days it felt cold and foreboding.

There was also a local rumour at the time that there was a tunnel under the cafe which led to the church – but she did not know whether anyone had ever established whether or not that was true.

No longer a food establishment, today the building houses an antique shop, and interestingly someone else said her aunt had run it for a while but never had any experiences there.

BURNHAM MARKET, Norfolk – CHURCH WALK

A witness wrote to me to tell me about a house she and her partner bought in 2003 in Church Walk, Burnham Market. It was a detached house originally built in the late 1920's, which was quite run down but had a lot of potential.

She called in her builder to help her assess the work that needed doing, and met with the vendor and the builder to discuss possibilities.

She was standing in the lounge with the vendor, who happened to be the granddaughter of the man who had originally built the property. They were discussing plans, when out of the corner of her eye she noticed the figure of an old man sat in a Windsor chair beside the fireplace puffing peaceably on a pipe.

Startled, she mentioned it to the vendor, who calmly replied that this was the ghost of her grandfather, who often appeared sitting in his favorite spot!

BURY ST EDMUNDS, Suffolk

As a child, my family and I lived for a time in a modern bungalow built in the grounds of the old prison, which at that time was known as The Fort, on Sicklesmere Road. The road itself was on the outskirts of the town at that time, and led into picturesque wheat fields which we often played in as children. At the front of the Fort, the old prison wall was still standing, and it was said to have been the site of the last public hanging in England - that of the Red Barn Murderer. Within the grounds, there were five detached bungalows as well as the remaining central tower of what had been the prison - a hexagonal building which was now converted into retirement flats. I remember being told that the various "wings" of the prison once radiated out from this central tower - hence its strange shape.

Our bungalow was the furthest in on the site, and seemed to have two figures haunting it. One was the figure of a lady with dark hair wearing a modern dress blouse and red skirt ensemble, who looked perfectly solid and real, according to our mother, who saw her twice. On both occasions, she saw the lady walk down our 'L' shaped hallway out of the corner of her eye, and would turn her head just in time to see her disappear into the bedroom at the end. She rushed after the figure, thinking a flesh and blood woman had just waltzed into the house, shouting words to the effect of "what on earth do you think you're doing?" on both occasions as she dashed into the bedroom mere seconds behind the woman - only to find the room empty.

The other was a small boy, of maybe six years old, wearing shorts and a polo shirt type top. He was again usually seen out of the corner of your eye, and often around the area of the bathroom, where he would usually be stood with his back towards you, so that you never saw his face. As soon as you turned to take a double take, he would disappear.

When I tried to find out whether anyone else had experienced anything at these properties, one lady recalled a story from her own childhood of a figure seen stepping out from the front wall of the prison, an architectural feature which is still there today. The figure walks a couple of steps, and then turns back into the wall and disappears.

She also explained that a house which she once owned in the street called Out Risby Gate was haunted. Her children were young at the time, and kept saying to her that they could see a man dressed in black in the house, which she of course dismissed as childish nonsense.

However, one day she was sitting in her lounge watching television when she heard the sound of running water coming from the nearby kitchen. Puzzled as to what she might have inadvertently left turned on, she got up and went to investigate. Finding nothing, she shrugged and walked back into the lounge – to find to her astonishment that her coffee table was suddenly and inexplicably covered in a thin pool of water from edge to edge! And yet there were no leaks in the ceiling and nothing that could have been knocked over.

On another night, as she was sitting in the lounge, her rug suddenly rose slightly off the ground as if a strong breeze had passed under it. Needless to say, the family decided that a move of house might be a good idea.

CALVERTON, Nottinghamshire – GEORGES LANE

There is a long standing local rumour that this lane in Calverton is haunted. The lane starts in the village, then winds its way out into the countryside, up a hill through sparsely wooded and gently rolling landscape until it meets Calverton Road. It is supposedly haunted by a figure in black.

The story goes that in the 1930s a Mr. Lawrence Bardill encountered the figure when returning from the Goose Fair close to midnight. He had reached the top of Georges Lane where it starts to descend down the hill towards the village, when something came out of a gateway he was passing. He described it as wearing a large hat, beneath which he glimpsed a prominent nose, and round its neck it wore a silver chain. He could not describe much else about the figure except to say that it was all in black.

Feeling apprehensive about who or what this was, Lawrence quickly crossed the road away from it, but to his horror it kept pace with him - even when he broke into a terrified run. After a few moments, it seemed to glide away into the night. The experience left him understandably shaken.

There are also stories that people see a figure materialise in the back seats of their car as they come down the hill - and that because of this taxi drivers are reluctant to agree to come out to Calverton at night for fear of what they might encounter.

It is reported that in 1992 a couple driving down the same hill suddenly saw a pair of legs, wearing what looked like riding breeches, run across the road in front of both their car and the bus which at that moment was coming from the opposite direction.

Another lady recounted how in her late teens she had tried to get a taxi back to Calverton from Nottingham in the early hours of one Sunday morning after a night out "on the town" with her friends, but her taxi driver insisted on taking a different route into the village to drop her off to avoid George's Lane. He told her that the previous occasion late at night that he had made that journey, he had dropped his fare off in the centre of the village before turning his cab around and starting the return journey up George's Lane, going uphill out of the village. Although his taxi was now empty of passengers, as he drove he heard a faint noise from the back seat which made him glance up and into his rearview mirror.

To his horror, he had seen the faint outline of what looked like an elderly man sitting on the back seat of his taxi. Not surprisingly, he was unwilling to risk a repeat performance.

A gentleman also recorded that his grandparents used to live at Hall Farm, at the bottom of Georges Lane. His grandmother used to tell the tale of how his grandfather had returned home late one evening after a trip to Arnold, clearly very shaken up and as white as a sheet. He had just seen the ghost as he drove down the lane.

Yet another lady recalled a friend of hers recounting how her friend, a very level headed, sensible person, was walking past the boundary wall of the old vicarage on a dark winter's night a few years ago when he noticed a figure in dark clothing, with its head down and large hat pulled down over its face walking towards him. The figure made no acknowledgement of her friend walking towards it, and did not veer its trajectory, so that in effect her friend was forced to step down off the path and allow it to pass or else risk a collision. Annoyed at the rudeness of the other person, her friend turned around to admonish him for the lack of manners only to discover to his horror that the figure had completely vanished.

I also found an account from 2003 of a lady who was babysitting one night at an address in Calverton, and at the end of her duty set off home driving up Georges Lane out of the village. It was a warm summer's evening, but as she drove she felt the car suddenly become icy cold, and someone seemed to push her driver's seat forward from behind. Terrified, she looked in her rearview mirror and saw a hooded figure in black there for a brief moment before it disappeared.

The only account I found where the apparition differed was a lady driving home late one evening on a cold foggy night who saw a man standing at the side of the road where Georges Lane passes Spindle Lane, who was wearing nothing but trousers and some sort of short sleeved light coloured top. As she passed him, and looked back puzzling what on earth he was doing out so late dressed so inappropriately for the weather, she realised that he had simply vanished.

When I asked locally, one lady told me that she lives in one of the cottages at the bottom end of Georges Lane, and was rudely awakened from slumber one night by what she can only describe as an "awful hooded thing" which momentarily seemed to have a hand around her neck before it promptly disappeared.

CAMELFORD, Cornwall.

I had a fascinating email from a gentleman in Germany, who told me about an experience during a family holiday to the UK in 1965. He and his mother stayed on a farm which rented rooms out to holidaymakers, which he recalled was about a twenty minute walk via a footpath across the fields from the town itself.

On one particular day, their hosts invited them along to go and visit their parents with them, since the older couple had recently bought a Manor House nearby. He was too young at the time to be able to remember the name of the Manor now, but recalled that it was made of light grey stone, was a very old building, possibly 13th Century, and sat in its own grounds of pastures and fields with a small stream running through.

The owner recounted to them that he had broken down one of the walls whilst renovating the property after moving in, and had discovered behind it the remains of a medieval kitchen still largely intact.

On some afternoons, they were told, the sounds of a battle could be heard emanating from the surrounding fields: and would be heard as clear sound, not faintly or in any way distorted.

The new lady of the manor had also been awoken one night to find a young woman standing in her bedroom. The apparition was holding what looked to be a basket of eggs, and the two stared at each other for a few long moments before the ghost faded away. Throughout the encounter, the family dogs, sleeping on the floor below the one her room was on, were frantically barking.

My correspondent explained to me that ever since, he has felt that hearing the experiences of these people he instinctively trusted as truthful has fundamentally altered his view of the world around us

CHERTSEY, Surrey - EASTWORTH ROAD

I spoke to one lady, who recalled vividly the problems that used to occur in her grandparents' home in Eastworth Road, Chertsey.

The house was a three bedroomed, semi-detached house, which had been built in the 1930s. Downstairs, there was a kitchen, a dining room, a lounge, and a lean-to style conservatory. Upstairs, there were three bedrooms, a small toilet room, and a bathroom. This style of having the toilet separate from the main bathroom was quite prevalent in Britain in houses of that period and later.

Our witness, Sarah, used to stay over at her grandparents' home quite often between the ages of 5 years old and around 10 years old, along with her older brother, because they were too young to be left on their own if their parents were going out.

Whenever they stayed over, they would sleep in the twin-bedded bedroom which had a small washbasin in one corner.

Sarah remembers frequently getting cross with her brother, because whenever she would put her belongings on the bed and leave the room, when she came back they would be lying scattered all over the floor. She was sure her brother was doing it to annoy her, but he would always deny having anything to do with it. On other occasions, some of the knick-knacks which sat on the shelf would also be flung onto the floor.

As the two siblings grew older, so they were allowed to sleep in separate rooms. Sarah vividly recalls that there was a large wardrobe in the corner of the room in a heavy old-fashioned dark wood - and that she was terrified of it. She remembers that every morning, when she awoke, she would be too scared to open her eyes - even to the extent of laying in her bed desperate to go to the toilet but not daring to move. She would lay there waiting until her grandparents would come to "wake her up" with a cup of tea - and once they were in the room she felt safe enough to start the day. She doesn't think they ever realised the real reason behind her apparent reluctance to get out of bed without her cup of tea.

Sarah also remembers that during the daytime, she would be afraid to go upstairs on her own to use the toilet. If she absolutely had to, she would rush up there and get all her business over and done with as quickly as possible so that she could rush back downstairs and not be alone.

She has a recollection of walking into the bedroom and seeing a lady in a big, dark, voluminous dress standing in the corner, her facial features hidden by what Sarah always recalled as a dark coloured parasol. She used to think of her as the Mary Poppins lady, because the shape of the clothing made her think of the popular film character. In later years, there was a large picture of a fairy or angel put in the corner where the lady used to stand, which she thinks was done with the aim of comforting her that there was nothing there.

By the time she was in her early teens, she would visit her grandparents often without her brother around - and yet still things would happen. She would do household chores for her grandparents in exchange for pocket money, and she has some vivid recollections of hoovering upstairs for them. On one occasion as she walked into one of the bedrooms and started pushing the hoover around, the door to the room suddenly slammed violently shut behind her, trapping her in the room and frightening her.

On another occasion, as she hoovered the landing between the bedrooms, suddenly all four doors slammed shut one after the other around her. The adults dismissed it as nothing to worry about, giving some vague explanation of there being air bricks at both sides of the property which caused a draught which in turn slammed the doors.

In time, her grandmother passed away and her grandfather was left living there on his own, and Sarah herself went away to university.

Sarah remembers visiting her surviving grandparent one day when she was home from university, and sitting with him in the lounge to have a cup of tea and a chat. As they sat there, suddenly overhead from the bedroom above came the sounds of heavy - and very distinct - footfalls. The steps were so pronounced and heavy that they were actually making the room's light fitting sway above Sarah's head. Turning to her grandfather she asked him in alarm who was upstairs, and he dismissed it, saying there was no-one up there and it was just the house settling: even as the footsteps rang out clearly above them. Not really believing him, she spoke to her mother about it, who airily dismissed her questions with "Oh that would have been the ghost of the monk - we used to regularly see him when I was a child". Her Mum admitted that whenever they saw the monk, he seemed to be walking on a different floor level to the one in the actual house.

She realises now, as an adult herself, that all the grown-ups at the time were fully aware of the phenomena, but deliberately staying completely calm about it (at least in her presence) in order not to frighten the children. She also wonders whether the woman in the black dress and parasol she recalls from her early childhood could maybe have been a monk in a dark coloured habit, but her young mind didn't know what a monk was and so chose a shape that it reminded her of – although of course that doesn't really account for the shape of a parasol.

On one occasion she visited her grandfather with her boyfriend of the time in tow, who happened to be a policeman. As they visited, the footsteps sounded again, and although her grandfather dismissed them again, the boyfriend was so convinced there must be an intruder by the heavy and tangible sound of the footsteps that he ran upstairs to confront them. He found nothing.

On another occasion, the whole family was there for a meal for a family occasion. The dining table had been set up and everyone was seated around it, enjoying their meal, when suddenly a ball of light floated slowly down the length of the table in front of all the astonished onlookers.

The years passed on, and Sarah married and had children, then later separated from her husband. As a single Mum now, she then bought a house a few doors down from where her grandparents used to live when they were alive. As soon as she moved in, a few strange things began to happen. She would hear really loud bangs coming either from outside or from elsewhere in the house, and inspection always revealed no apparent cause for the sound.

On other occasions, pools of water would randomly be found around the house – one time in the middle of the sofa bed, on other occasions in the middle of the conservatory floor. Despite extensive investigation, they could never find any leaks or obvious natural causes, and the pools would not reform once cleared up.

One night, in bed, Sarah heard the loud bang again, and this time instead of getting up to investigate she stayed in bed and just shouted out "What do you want!"

She has never dared repeat that, because early the next morning when she got out of bed to go and wake her own children, one of her children's colouring pens was on the floor with the lid off and unintelligible scrawling on the floor – as if something had tried to answer her.

She did have a ghost hunter visit the house, and he brought with him an EMF meter and a Spirit Box.

EMF meters record the levels of Electromagnetic fields – and are commonly used by electrical engineers as everything electrical gives off an EM Field. It has been shown that a high EM field can result in hallucination type response in humans, and there is also a theory that spirits disturb the natural EM field as they pass, so that sudden spikes or dips in a baseline recording can show that a spirit is near. They are often seen on television ghost hunting shows with flashing lights to indicate an increase in the field level, although the standard industrial ones tend to simply have either a digital readout or dial (not as visually effective for TV viewing of ghost hunts in darkened rooms!).

A spirit box works by rapidly scanning backwards and forwards across the bandwidth of radio frequencies, never pausing long enough to actually lock onto the signal from a particular radio station. The theory here is that a spirit can manipulate the radio field and cause the box to "throw out" random words in response to questions asked.

In this instance, Sarah says that she distinctly heard her grandfather's voice through the device calling "Sarah, Sarah!"

The EMF meter also came up with some very high readings.

She was going to have the house "cleansed", but actually the activity just gradually died down, and today the house is a very calm and peaceful place, with the river running at the bottom of the garden.

Out of curiosity, she has checked to see if there was a building on the site prior to the houses being built which might have had a different floor level – but as far as she can ascertain, there was never a building there as this is actually an area of flood plain. There was however an abbey not far away, Chertsey Abbey, which was often attacked in raids by the Danes, so the presence of a monk is entirely plausible. Sadly very little evidence of the Abbey remains today, since the Dissolution in the reign of King Henry VIII.

CIRENCESTER, Wiltshire – GLOUCESTER STREET

A witness wrote to me to tell me that sometime in the 1980's, herself, her husband, and their young children moved into a house on Gloucester Street, in Cirencester. It was one of the old stone terraced cottages along that street. Parts of the road are built along the same route as an old Roman Road, and a Roman cemetery was located nearby.

One night, in around 1989, she awoke from her sleep needing to pop to the loo. Moving quietly so as not to disturb the rest of the family, she carefully got out of bed and tiptoed out to visit the bathroom. Returning, she climbed back into bed and shut her eyes, but instantly snapped them open again as something caught her attention.

Standing in her bedroom was a young girl wearing some sort of floor length gown. The dress had a square yoke across the shoulders and upper chest, with gathers of material below that. She had long dark wavy hair which reached down past her shoulders - and most horribly, both eyes had been gouged out: and the eyeballs were laying on her cheeks still attached to the empty sockets. The witness believes the ghost might have been that of a murdered girl.

CLOPHILL, Bedfordshire

This small and picturesque Bedfordshire village makes its second appearance in one of my books, as it seems to have its fair share of haunted areas! Whilst researching for "The Roadmap of British Ghosts" I was also told about these other two hauntings, which I did not include there because they did not fit into the "theme" of that book.

A lady wrote to me to tell me that in the 1980's, she and her family were living in one of the properties along Bedford Road in the village. One dull winter's afternoon, she took her baby son upstairs for his nap and settled him quietly down on her bed. Lulling him to sleep took a few minutes, and the peace and quiet also lulled her into dozing off alongside him. Like all young mums, she knew that it was a good idea to catch forty winks if she could while he was also sleeping.

A short while later, she startled awake due to a noise which had caught her attention as something she had never heard before. Sitting upright in alarm, she realised that dusk had started to fall (it being mid-afternoon in winter), and that the sound which had awoken her was all the small ornaments arranged along her bedroom windowsill jumping up and down in a seemingly frantic way – tapping out a staccato rhythm which had startled her out of slumber.

In the same moment of startled wakefulness, she also realised that in her tiredness, she had rolled over onto the baby – and a few more minutes may well have resulted in her inadvertently smothering him had she not been awoken by her oddly behaving ornaments. To this day, she feels strongly that someone or something warned her in time to save his life that day.

I was also told about one of the local pubs – "The Stone Jug" by another correspondent. She worked as a part time barmaid there over recent years, up until 2018, and was convinced the pub was haunted by one of the previous landlords.

She had worked for him when he was alive, and was used to hearing his footsteps in the private rooms above the bar and the sound of his dog's paws clicking on the flooring as he followed his master around – and she still heard these familiar sounds long after he had died. Another habit of the previous landlord when still living had been to hum tuneless little ditties under his breath as he worked around the bar and cellars – and for years afterwards she would still hear those tuneless little snippets as if her old colleague was still going about his daily routines.

COCKENZIE, East Lothian, Scotland

A lady wrote to me to tell me of her experience in the early 1970s when she was a young woman, not yet married or with a family of her own. At that time, the Miners' Industrial Action Strikes were happening up and down the country, and was the subject of much of the talk amongst locals with Cockenzie being a working port town which had intrinsic links with the export and import of the mining industry.

On the night in question, she and her pals had been on a night out, and were now making their way home. Her girlfriends had walked with her down as far as the main road just past the power station, where they had left her to complete the short last leg of her journey on her own.

She stated, "I was not scared as there was a man walking a wee bit in front of me". As she neared the row of shops in the middle of Cockenzie, she noticed another man leaning casually against a side wall. Cautious at first, since she was now a woman walking at night on her own, she took a good look at him as she approached.

She realised almost straight away that she recognised him – it was the janitor from her school days. He was an older man, and was leaning against the wall smoking a cigarette. He was particularly recognisable because of the eye patch he always wore.

As soon as his identification really kicked into her brain – she screamed and jumped involuntarily sideways into the road with shock. As she explained to me, had any vehicles been approaching at that moment, she would have put herself in very real danger of being knocked down. So violent and vocal was her reaction that the man who had been walking along in front of her turned around and called to ask if she was OK. She turned to look again at the man smoking his cigarette – but he had disappeared. She was not surprised – she had screamed and jumped when she recognised the old janitor because she knew already that he had in fact been killed in a motorcycle accident along this same stretch of road some years earlier.

COVENTRY, Warwickshire – BURNABY ROAD

My correspondent Jake from Baldock (see earlier entry), also told me about an experience he had in a 1930s style end of terrace house in Burnaby Road in Coventry.

He was supposed to start living there to share-rent it with a friend, but he was quite worried about moving into it because it just didn't feel right to him: As fate would have it, various unrelated circumstances changed for the two friends, and she ended up living there for around two years from 2002 to 2004 without him sharing the property with her as they had originally planned.

Nevertheless, they were good friends, so he spent a lot of time round at the house visiting with her during the period she lived there. He described how it was one of those houses that somehow always feels gloomy and dark, even though there were enough windows of a good enough size to let in plenty of natural light. He said it had a weird way of muffling sound, so that silence in that house felt as if it was louder than white noise, and as if it was muffling or muting sounds coming from the outside.

His friend suffered from quite a run of bad luck whilst living in the house, and eventually she decided to pack everything up and return to her native home in Scotland. In order to help, Jake agreed to collect the key from her and take it back in to the letting agency. He needed to pop back into the house anyway to give it a last check over and pick up a couple of items of his own which had been left there.

This meant going into the cupboard under the stairs to collect the stuff he had stored there, and it was both night time, and the power had already been turned off - so the property was in complete darkness. Jake had to crouch down to reach back into the cupboard, and as he fumbled around in the gloom, his back was facing the open doors of the living room and dining room. Suddenly, and quite distinctly, he heard someone whisper "Help Me!"

As he put it, "Well I was out the front door like my ass was on fire. Took me 10 minutes to get back up the courage to go to the front door and shut it."

I asked locally whether anyone knew anything of the property, but no-one came forward. There was apparently a different house further along the same road, nearer to the pub, which lay empty for some time until it was almost derelict. That one had a reputation of being haunted by the sound of footsteps upstairs and going up the stairs themselves.

CRANBROOK, Kent

A witness wrote to me to tell me about the horrible experience she had when viewing a property she was thinking of buying, just off the High Street in Cranbrook, Kent.

She and her daughter had gone together to view the property one afternoon, in full daylight. At first, her impression was that the cottage was really lovely, and might be just what she was looking for. Starting to feel excited about the prospect, she walked ahead of her daughter and hurried up the stairs to look at the attic bedroom.

To her own astonishment and absolute fear, she was greeted by an awful sight at the top of the stairs. High up on the wall above the well of the staircase there was some sort of gas or electric meter, with some fairly hefty sized pipes emanating from it. Hanging from one of these pipes was the shadowy form of a man - who was actively looking at her with a very angry countenance!

Needless to say, she did not put in an offer to buy the property but made her excuses and hurriedly left.

Some months later, she was talking with another local lady, and the chat turned to discussing a photo of the cottage. This second lady, with no prior knowledge of our witness' experience, told her that what happened there had been such a shame. When our witness asked her to explain, the other lady told her that a previous owner had committed suicide by hanging himself in the stairwell. This second lady had actually been the one to find him - and described how dreadful it was that at first she had thought he was just standing on the stairs before she realised that she was witnessing a dead body and a final act of desperation.

DALSTON HALL, Cumbria

Sarah [a pseudonym] wrote to me to tell me her story about her experiences when she lived in this wonderful old hall. The house was built around 1500 by John Dalston, as a magnificent residence for his family. A west wing was added in around 1556, and the beautiful building remained in the same family for a couple of centuries and through many generations. It finally changed hands in 1761. After several changes of owners, more extensions and changes to the facade, it was finally converted into a luxury hotel in 1971. From the outside, it looks a bit like a castle, set in very attractive grounds.

Sarah's family moved into the warden's house around 1962 or 1963, when her father became the warden of the estate. She explained how the estate has a long driveway, which at the end forks left to go to the Warden's House, and to the right to go to the Hall itself. At that time, the Hall was being used for a residential training centre, and they would therefore have a number of guests staying there at any one time. Both her father, her mother, and also herself worked for the Hall.

Sarah had been working in the Hall one late shift, and was walking back along the drive to go home. It was around 10pm in the evening, and although it was autumn, the night was clear and not too cold. The driveway was unlit, but there was enough starlight and moonlight that she could see her way quite clearly, and in any case she was very familiar with the route and could easily navigate it in the dark without any problems.

She explained, "As I reached the fork and turned towards our house, a hooded figure came from the house, crossed silently across the gravel drive in front of me and merged into the hedge. My mum was very fond of her duffle coat so my first response was to think that it was her coming to meet me, with the hood of her coat up."

Sarah only realised that she was seeing the infamous Grey Lady ghost which haunts the Hall when the figure disappeared into the hedge. The apparition was only about a hundred yards from her, so quite clearly seen.

On another occasion, whilst driving home as a passenger in her boyfriend's car at about 10.30pm one evening along the same stretch of the driveway, she suddenly felt an overwhelming sense of fear and that something truly evil was close by: she described it as a seriously frightening experience even though there was nothing to physically see or hear. She was about 17 years old at the time, and she became so distressed by the sense of evil all around her that her boyfriend stopped the car to try and help her.

The last encounter Sarah told me about was one where she and some school friends sneaked into the room above the Library in the Hall itself, and decided to conduct an Ouija board. At first nothing seemed to happen, but then one of her friends became very disturbed, saying she could sense something evil close by her pushing at her mind. The poor girl became so frightened that she fainted.

DEVIZES, Wiltshire

Just on the outskirts of this very picturesque old town, there is a canal with a long flight of locks, called the Caen Hill Locks.

A lady wrote to tell me her story of walking beside these locks once when she lived in nearby Mayenne Place. Obviously, with such a beautiful sight right on her very doorstop, it was somewhere she often walked.

One lovely sunny day, she decided to go out to the shops, and thought it would be nice to walk the long way round, by the canal, to enjoy the beautiful day. She was strolling along watching the ducks and swans on the canal, and feeling happy and at peace with the world.

As she came close to the town bridge, she noticed a beautiful Red Setter dog trotting towards her. Although he passed close enough that she could have reached down and petted him, he did not stop to make a fuss. She turned to watch him go past her, wondering whether he should try and catch him as no one seemed to be with him and he might be lost.

However, the point quickly became moot, since even as she watched him he faded from sight and disappeared!

Later that day she visited with her mother, and told her about the strange experience she had down by the canal. Her mother told her that there used to be an older man who walked his beloved Red Setter by the canal most days until the dog died.

EARDISLAND, Herefordshire

Jake, a witness from both Baldock and Coventry earlier in the book, also told me that he and his friends once hired a self-catering holiday home in Eardisland, Herefordshire, called The Manor House. The property is actually a 17th century building which has been sensitively restored and refurbished, and makes for a pleasant getaway.

It was in the later part of the year 2009, and there was a large group of friends gathering together to celebrate the tenth wedding anniversary for one of the couples in the group.

It was a long weekend type of celebration, and Jake and his partner were assigned the attic bedroom in the property for the duration of their trip. It was a beautiful property in stunning surroundings, but as they walked into their bedroom to put down their luggage, my witness explained that to him, the room didn't feel very welcoming or comfortable, although he would be hard pushed to put his finger on why. As it was an attic room, the ceiling was peaked with steeply sloping sides, so the double bed was positioned in the centre of the room, and there was a painting of the Madonna and child hanging on the wall at the head of the bed.

He didn't want to spook or alarm his partner, so he said nothing about his misgivings, and they spent the first evening having a great time with all their friends. Eventually it was time to retire to bed, and Jake laid on his side with his back to his partner, with his legs slightly apart and bent at the knee. As he lay there with his eyes shut, trying to doze, he distinctly felt the bed between his legs dip down as if someone quite heavy had just sat on the end of the mattress. He looked down, wondering if his partner was moving about, but there was nothing to be seen, and the weight lifted again even as he watched. Terrified, but still not wanting to make it difficult for his unsuspecting partner, he shut his eyes. To his horror, he felt the bedclothes being tugged and pulled from the bottom of the bed, and had to hold tightly onto them to stop the movement.

His partner had never stirred throughout the entire encounter, and Jake was unsurprisingly too frightened to open his eyes again and look to see if there was anything visible present.

Once the weekend was over and they had returned home, he did look the property up online, and found that the building had been visited by at least one paranormal research team, who reported hearing loud bangs, seeing light anomalies, and people in the group finding the location was atmospheric with a brooding atmosphere – "particularly the room with the portrait of the Madonna and child".

EAST KIRKBY, Lincolnshire – EAST KIRKBY AIRFIELD

One lady wrote in to tell me about a very curious experience she had in 1999, which although not exactly a "haunting", I have included because it is fascinating in its oddness.

At that time, she was living in Skegness. She had grown up in Spilsby though, and was hoping to move back to the area. Her grandfather had lived in Old Bolingbroke for his whole life, and on this particular day she had decided to pop over and visit him after she had been on a trip to Boston. She took the route which cut across the old runways at the back of East Kirkby Airfield. It was a route she often took, and she knew it very well.

She described how just as you drive onto the old airfield land, you negotiate a sharp right hand bend with a large house on the left of it. The road then opens up and runs straight across the old tarmac flats. On this particular day, as she drove around the bend, she suddenly noticed a beautiful cottage on the right hand side which she had never noticed before. It really caught her eye, especially as she was hoping to move back into the area, so she slowed right down to take a good look at it.

She thought it looked like it might be a converted ban, built of an attractive red brick, and had small leaded windows with some sort of greenery growing up the brickwork and curling around the windows themselves.

It stood very close to the road, but on its own and with pretty gardens either side. It had a For Sale board up, and she felt quite excited at the look of it. She was a little puzzled that she had not noticed it all the other times she had driven that road, but dismissed that thought as likely to be because she had never been actively looking at buying a house in the area before so probably had not paid much attention to it the way she was now.

She didn't have a mobile phone or camera to take a picture of the For Sale sign with, and by the time she had visited with her grandfather for a while, and then driven on home to Skegness, she couldn't for the life of her remember the name of the Estate Agent which had been on the For Sale board, so that she could follow up on it.

So the very next day, she persuaded her partner to drive out with her so that she could show him the house and so that they could get the details and follow up on it if he thought it was as promising looking as she did. They drove the same route she had the day before, travelling in the same direction, and although she was sure she knew exactly where it was - there was absolutely nothing there. No house. No building. No sign there ever had been.

Confused, she drove them all up and down the road and around the surrounding area, thinking maybe she had been mistaken in remembering where it was. The house was nowhere to be found. She has driven the route many times since, and has never found the house she wanted so much to look at buying.

EATHORPE, Warwickshire – THE PLOUGH INN

This pleasant early Victorian building has stone floors and beams, giving it a charming atmosphere. My same witness as from Coventry and Baldock earlier in the book, Jake, once worked as a barman, many years ago before he was married.

He distinctly recalls one night after closing time, whilst he was clearing up the bar area, he felt someone poke him hard on his shoulder, just near the edge of his collarbone. The poke was accompanied by a tingling feeling as of static electricity, and made him stop in astonishment and catch his breath for a moment.

On another occasion, one of his friends drinking in the bar area watched a white figure glide across one corner of the room and disappear through a door – without other people who were present seeming to notice it.

Looking at the property online reveals that it has a reputation today of having a slightly malign ghost resident there, who is known for poking and pushing people! A lady working there had once reported that whilst mopping the floor, she was at first prodded with a sharp finger, which poked her hard in the shoulder and then given a quite violent push. This has also allegedly happened to other people working in the cellar area, and some people have reported seeing the outline of a person walk across the bar and disappear through a door. My witness Jake is certain he had never seen these reports online before – it had never occurred to him to check the pub online before talking to me.

The pub is currently closed, and is undergoing extensive refurbishment with intention of opening as soon as possible. The current owner, Lee, told me that although they have only owned the property for around six months, since early 2019, they have already had a few strange things happen which they can't quite explain. On a couple of occasions chairs have moved or creaked slightly, as if someone had just sat down, or a door has opened itself when it was definitely left shut.

FLITWICK, Bedfordshire - THE RIDGEWAY

I met this next witness over a coffee in the nearby market town of Ampthill in a small and crowded coffee shop, over hot chocolate and crumpets. It seemed slightly incongruous to be talking about ghosts in such a mundane setting - but then again, so many paranormal encounters do take place in otherwise utterly mundane settings - so perhaps it was fitting.

Our witness, a well-spoken lady who had brought with her a helpful folder of photographs of the house, explained to me that she and her husband had bought the house in the short street called "The Ridgeway" in Flitwick as newlyweds, with the intention of making it their first family home. It was the mid 1970's, and they had moved from their first home, a flat, into this wonderfully spacious old house, most of which had been built in the 1860's.

Originally, it would have been a typical double fronted house with the entry door in the middle of the front facade, flanked by spacious windows into probably a lounge and drawing room. It had a basement area as well. At the time when it was built, it would actually have stood in the small hamlet of Dennel End which has long since been forgotten and subsumed into the small town of Flitwick, and in its day it would have been quite an imposing property for its location, with attendant outbuildings and probably some land, where now there are other houses and buildings crowding around.

By the time the young couple bought it, the property had been added to numerous times over the years, including a large extension on one side built in the 1920s. It had seen various incarnations over the decades, including a period as a shop during the Second World War. It was in quite a sad state of repair when they made the purchase, and they had high plans of how they would renovate it to turn it into the spacious home they envisaged starting their family in.

When they moved in, they were thrilled at how much space they suddenly owned, and decided that this would make it easier to renovate since they could work room by room - thus keeping the mess and clutter associated with the renovation confined to distinct areas whilst they lived in other rooms. They decided to start with one of the beautiful front rooms - stripping it completely bare of all fixtures and fittings and then strip the walls right back to the original plaster. They were excited to be planning the lovely dining room it would become.

They had not long been in the house when the first instance occurred. They had just finished stripping out the front room, and had retired for the night to their bedroom, which was directly above the room they were working on. No sooner had they settled into bed, tired from the day's labour, when they were startled back into full wakefulness by the sound of an almighty crash from the room directly below them.

Shooting out of bed, the young couple were thoroughly alarmed, wondering what on earth could have toppled over - the sound was as if some heavy item of furniture had fallen. As they hurriedly made their way downstairs to investigate, they both agreed that the sound had definitely seemed to emanate from the room below theirs: the room they had just stripped bare of any and all furniture.

They could find nothing disturbed in the bare dining room to-be, so in puzzlement they widened their search to the rest of the house, and eventually even outside, where they found the night air still, quiet, and undisturbed by any commotion.

They could not think of any explanation for the loud noise which had made them bolt out of bed. Giving up, they retired for the rest of the night and largely forgot about the incident.

The next night, our witness was making her way up the stairs intending to head to the bathroom, and had reached as far as the half landing when she thought she saw a shadow cross the full landing above her and go into one of the bedrooms. Knowing that no-one else was upstairs, she tried to rationalise it, assuring herself it must have been a cloud shadow momentarily darkening the windows from outside and causing her to think she had seen a shadow move - but in reality she knew deep down that something had just moved in the periphery of her vision.

Over the next few weeks, she became increasingly aware that the staircase always felt like it had a presence on it - a presence that was carefully watching her come and go and which left her feeling slightly uneasy. On more than one occasion, she thought she saw the same shadow moving in the periphery of her vision as she ascended - almost as if someone was deliberately moving out of her line of sight.

Eventually, on one particular day she decided enough was enough, and stopped stock still on the half landing. Feeling slightly daft, but at the same time feeling it was the right thing to do, she spoke out loud to what she now felt was a presence they were sharing the house with. She told it that there was nothing for it to be worried about, that although they were making a lot of changes in the house they were just renovating it so that it could become a family home once more, and that they were planning to stay and raise their children there.

It seemed to work, because things quietened down and there were no more incidences. Time passed, and in due course the young couple had their first child, a son, followed 18 months later by their second child, a daughter. Our witness became a stay-at-home Mum, as was very much the norm in those days, and found herself with long hours on her hands and only the children and house to occupy her mind. She relied quite heavily, like most young mums, on a network of ladies in the same position, who formed friendships and bonds and worked together to raise the children and help one another out. One such young mum became a particularly close friend, and the pair would often spend time in one another's company.

Now our young couple had often commented on a strange cold spot that was in their lounge, just by the sofa and near the door into the room. It was a distinct "column" of chilled air - about a foot or so in diameter and rising from floor to ceiling in a noticeable block which you could actually feel by passing your hands through it. The column of cold air never wavered or moved, and the young husband had often tried to bring all his logic to bear on it and try to find what the physical cause of it was – never to any avail.

When the friend visited, she commented almost immediately upon this cold spot in the room, confirming that it was a palpable thing and not something the couple were imagining. She then went upstairs to use the bathroom, and when she came back downstairs tried very delicately to ask about the history of the house and what it had been before – harping on the subject until the owner commented to her "you've seen something on the stairs, haven't you?"

The friend had also noticed the shadow moving, the same as our witness, but when she turned to look fully at it, for a moment she saw a male figure, about 5'6" and seeming to be in his mid-fifties or so. He was wearing a soft cap, dark blue trousers, and an old looking sports jacket. She said that she could not clearly see him – he was sort of "smudged out" to look at, so she couldn't really describe his features, but he was gone in an instance. The same friend saw him several more times over the years, but never so clearly as that first time.

When their son was about three years old, and a happy, chattering toddler, he had an imaginary friend. His friend was called George, and the young lad would want George to be allowed to have a place setting at the table next to him or be allowed to play with him – in the way small children often do in a phase they go through. The couple didn't think much about it, until one Saturday morning when they were trying to have a rare lie in.

Their baby daughter was still asleep in her room in her crib, and they could hear their young lad happily playing and chattering away to himself in his room, so they snuggled down for just a few moments of undisturbed peace – a commodity prized above all else by most young parents.

Their bliss didn't last long though, because their son came trotting into the room chattering that he wanted George to come and talk with them.

Except, he was holding his arm up in the air as if holding the hand of an adult man, and tugging as if trying to pull a reluctant adult to follow him. The young husband was utterly horrified at the sight of his baby son apparently conversing with an invisible male adult, and without thinking jumped out of bed, snatched his young son up in his arms and slammed the bedroom shut on "George" - only then realising his mistake and crying out "Oh my God - the baby". His wife was the one who got out of bed and went to calmly retrieve their perfectly happy baby daughter from their crib - but she said her husband remained shaken by the incident for some time, because the idea of the son having an imaginary play friend was one thing - but for that friend to turn out to be an adult male when they knew an adult male ghost had been seen in their house was just too much for him - and not something he has ever really wanted to discuss since.

After that incident they lived there for another three years, but "George" seemed to go away, and the shadows were hardly ever seen - although the cold column in the lounge remained. Their cat continued to react to that throughout the time they lived there - skirting carefully round it and sometimes staring at it and hissing with her fur fluffed up.

The very last time anything happened was shortly after they had put the house on the market and were getting ready to pack up and leave. She caught a glimpse of "George" one last time on the stairs, looking slightly distressed. It was the clearest she had ever actually seen him - but even then his colours were sort of muted and again there was the "smudging" effect, meaning it wasn't like looking clearly at someone: so that her sense of him looking distressed was more a feeling than something visual. She spoke out loud to him - reassuring him that another family were moving in and the house would go on and he would be alright to stay there. She left with the feeling that her words had given the spirit a sense of calm..

GLASGOW, Great Western Road - GLASGOW GENERAL HOSPITAL.

A lady told me about an incident that happened to her own mother, when the mother was herself a young lady working as a Nurse at this hospital. It would have been sometime around the late 1940s.

At this time, most people did not have transport of their own, and of course the bus service only operated at certain times of the day and evening, so the staff at the hospital working the graveyard shifts often had difficulty getting into work or home from work at the unsociable times they needed to be travelling. To try and mitigate against the problem, there was a rule that they could use any of the empty rooms to sleep in either before their shift started or after it ended, whilst they waited for it to be time for the buses to run again.

My witness explained, "Mum was in a side room on her own, sleeping on what she described as a big heavy iron-framed hospital bed. She said she awoke suddenly, feeling inexplicably terrified. She had an overwhelming urge to get out of that room, but when she tried to get off the bed it started to shake violently. She said she couldn't get off it. She tried to scream for help but no sound came out."

Her mother always said that the horrible experience seemed to last for an age, with her struggling and failing to get off the shaking bed. Eventually she did manage to get to her feet, and make a run for the door.

As she got there, one of her older nursing colleagues arrived at the door as well. Weirdly, although she had not heard anything or anyone cry out, this older nurse told our witness' Mum that she had suddenly felt an overwhelming urge to come to the room as someone needed help!

Both nurses peered into the room - and the sturdy bed had shaken itself away from the wall and into the middle of the floor. Curiously, this side room was one which had originally been used to give electric shock therapy to patients with mental health issues: although thankfully this barbaric practice was no longer in use by the time this incident occurred.

GREAT WAKERING, Essex - HIGH

STREET

There has probably been some sort of community built on this ancient site and surrounding area since at least the seventh century, since there is record of a monastery close to here which enshrined the bones of two saints, Aethelred and Aethelberht, who according to legend had been murdered at Eastry when there used to be a royal palace there. (This was in the time when England was actually a conglomerate of small Kingdoms, not one united one like it is now). According to the legend, the two princes were murdered as part of a struggle over who would succeed the throne, and their bodies were concealed under the Throne itself. They became Saints because their resting place was revealed by a Divine Light which shone down on them.

It is perhaps not surprising, with such a long history, that the village itself seems to be very active in terms of supernatural phenomena.

One lady told me that many years ago when her son was only two years old, she used to live in one of the properties along the High Street. Her son could often be heard in his bedroom chatting away, and he would say that he was talking to the "policeman" in his room. As the family held strong Christian beliefs they never encouraged any thought of spirits or ghosts, but she has always been puzzled by the fact that the properties were, originally, built to house the local constabulary. Something which her two year old son could not possibly have known...

Another lady told me that her family also used to occupy a property along the High Street, and that they had an awful lot of strange occurrences there. As a child, her sleep was often disturbed by things in the night, and she would draw pictures of what she saw and show them to her mother. She always felt that there was a particular presence in the hallway.

Another woman said that she too had once lived in a cottage along the High Street. They had activity which was much more "poltergeist" like in nature. A poltergeist is the popular name for a spirit or entity which moves objects: the name itself derives from German and means "noisy spirit". In this particular cottage, objects would often move on their own accord. On one occasion, the lampshade was moved, and on another a cutlery draw was taken out and moved to the other side of the kitchen whilst she and her husband lay in bed.

On another occasion, whilst trying to take a nice relaxing bath one evening, she suddenly felt as if someone had taken hold of her and was trying to push her underneath the water. Shaken by that negative experience, she and her husband decided to ask for the help of a medium. This medium told them that a previous family were still resident in the cottage and were intent on causing mischief. They decided discretion was the better part of valour and put the cottage up for sale immediately.

Yet another witness told me that for a while they used to live in a cottage in Great Wakering, and that she often used to see the form of an elderly gentleman in her kitchen. He would seem to be sitting peaceably in the armchair next to her oven, but the sight still used to freak her out. He would often appear, calmly sitting there, when she had to go and put the bins out in the dark – a chore she hated doing as she had always been afraid of the dark.

They eventually found out that he was a previous resident of the property, called Albert, who had died in his armchair by in the same corner where he now sat next to her oven. Eventually, she came to take comfort in his presence, because it felt almost as if he were watching out for her because he knew she was afraid to be alone in the dark.

One correspondent told me that they live in Exhibition Lane in Great Wakering, having moved there in 1989. He explained, "We have had numerous occurrences over the years, including actual sightings, speech, being actively observed, things moving, etc. I have had experiences in the past which at times have been quite frightening but in this house there has never been any feeling of malicious intent and we have no worries about what may be here."

He told me that the very first time something happened was on the actual night they moved into the property. He said, "We had an old fashioned divan bed with a solid base. We had both been asleep for a little while when we were awoken by the sound of the base being kicked. We both woke up and saw a figure backing away from the bed, ducking under the door and away down the stairs. The figure was outlined in gold light. The best comparison would be "Dancing Man" from the credits of the old grey whistle test, if you are old enough to remember that".

(If you want to look at that image, search on YouTube for the theme tune to that popular TV programme – the figure on it became known as "star kicker" and was outlined by golden stars.)

It also quickly became apparent that the brand new pair of Doc Martin Boots which he had bought for work and which he was wearing the day they moved had disappeared, and they have never been seen since.

They owned two wardrobes when they moved in, which were too big to be moved up the stairs. In the end, the only choice was to dismantle them, carry them upstairs that way, and then reassemble them in situ. Although he rebuilt them that same day, one piece was never found – a plinth rail. They never really thought much about it, just assuming it had gotten lost and accidentally thrown out in the upheaval of the day – until the day five years later when it made a reappearance, casually leaning against the wardrobe door.

Not long after they moved in, some friends visited for the weekend, bringing their young children with them. Everybody enjoyed the visit, but after it was over and the family had left they telephoned to ask whether their daughters small tooth brush had been accidentally left behind. They assured their guests it had not – after carefully checking all around for it. About ten years later, my witness got up one morning, walked into the bathroom to begin his morning ablutions, and found a small pink toothbrush resting on the lip of the bathroom sink.

About a year after they moved in, probably in the late summer of 1990, the couple went out on a Saturday afternoon to one of the local pubs. However, whilst they were there, a summer thunderstorm blew up, and they decided to hurry home before it hit as they were not dressed to be caught out in a rainstorm. Arriving home, the husband decided he might as well make a start on cooking dinner, but seeing as it was still hot and very humid due to the approaching storm, he left the back door open to try and let some cooling air in.

As he moved about the kitchen preparing vegetables and getting down pots and pans, he was disturbed suddenly by the figure of a man walking in through the open door, past him as he stood astonished, and on up the cottage stairs. Needless to say, the second he got over his astonishment he dashed up the stairs to follow the figure - but there was no-one to be found. He said that the figure "looked to be dressed as a labourer, from a long time ago, flat cap, scarf tied at the throat, worn out suit & overcoat".

In that same year, he was working upstairs putting new wallpaper up in their bedroom. He explained, "I was cutting round a light switch, it was again hot and I turned my head to wipe sweat off of my forehead as it was running in my eyes, as I turned my head I clearly saw a woman, intently watching me, as though trying to see what I was doing."

He said that she was wearing a brown patterned dress, full length, and pulled in tight at the waist, with her hair piled on top of her head in an old fashioned "bun". Astonished, he quickly turned to look fully at her, but she had vanished. He never saw her again.

He did, however, see the male apparition again. He remembers clearly that it was in 1996, because the European football tournament was on and he had deliberately made sure to come home from work in time to watch the evening game. He was just getting washed up in the bathroom ready to settle down to his evening's entertainment, when the same figure walked past the bathroom door and away down the staircase. He said it was clearly recognisable as the same figure, but this time it was somehow "more blurry".

During the time that they lived there, they fitted a bolt to the outside of the bathroom door, so that they could shut it and lock it whenever they went out, to prevent their adventurous pet cats from getting in and causing mischief. On one occasion his wife was in the bath, when she heard a "snick" sound and found herself suddenly bolted inside the room! Fortunately her husband happened to be at home, so when she called out he was able to go up and rescue her. They were the only two people in the building at the time. On another occasion, his wife came home to find that she could not get in through the front door because someone had put the chain on.

He also stated, "I can think of two occasions when visitors have heard what they though was me whispering to them, but both times I was nowhere near, and when I asked them they could not remember anything that was said, just that they had heard a voice."

Another person wrote to tell me that she herself has skills as a medium, and moved into a property along the HIgh Street in 2018. She told me, "We had to do a lot of work to the property. The back of the house has an extension and when I was walking through the new area into the bathroom I felt really anxious almost as though someone was watching me. I tuned into the feeling and felt as though it was a trapped spirit of a young boy aged in his early teens. A friend of mine who is also a medium came round and I asked her to tune in but did not make her aware of what I had sensed and she picked up the same thing.

"I spoke to him and he told me that at the back of the house there used to be an outhouse or outside toilet and his father, a very stern man, used to lock his little son in there. The boy was fair or ginger haired and was very sensitive and his father was trying to make a man of him. When he passed to spirit it was quite sudden and a shock to him as he was still quite young. He would not go into the arms of his parents after he passed because he was frightened so he remained an earth bound spirit. I spent some time talking to him and letting him know it was ok and during the rescue a close school friend came for him and he went into the light. It was lovely. My house is now a warm tranquil space."

Another lady recalled living in New Road as a six year old child in the mid-1980s. She would often see the apparition of an old lady sitting on the end of her bed at night. The lady was short, with grey hair, and would rock backwards and forwards as if distressed in some way. The ghost appeared on most nights for the three year period that our witness used the room as her bedroom. I think this might be the bravest witness of all

– I'm not sure I could go up to bed every night for three years knowing I would see something sitting on my bed!

Another gentleman told me that he had once spoken with a former resident of Great Wakering, who told him that his brother had died tragically when they were young. He told our witness that for a while, the spirit of his brother "came back" and plagued the family by throwing things around in their property on the High Street. Eventually, a priest was called in to say a blessing and help him to go to his rest.

In another house on the High Street, I am told, one lady's mother used to do the cleaning. The owner of the house told the mother that she had once seen something which was reminiscent of the popular perception of a "grim reaper" hovering over one of her daughters as she was sleeping in the far end bedroom. Although the mother screamed at whatever it was and made it go away, for a while she could not awaken her child. She never let the children sleep in that room again.

Yet another resident told me how her mother used to tell the tale of the house she lived in on the High Street in Great Wakering, where the lights would often switch themselves on or off. She also used to tell about ancient old tunnels which are said to run under the town, and where the ghost of a man with a lantern haunts.

HADLEIGH, Suffolk – HIGH STREET

Another village which I got a lot more than I bargained for when I asked whether anyone knew of the haunted property in the HIgh Street (following an earlier lead I had been given) was Hadleigh in Suffolk. Over a dozen people responded, and as one of them wryly pointed out, it would have been easier to ask which properties were NOT haunted!

To try and succinctly list it out, essentially I was told of a ghost in the Town Hall, two flats above shops that are haunted, the White Lion pub, and at least five of the shops and other properties along the High Street.

One person recalled a member of their family seeing the one in the Town Hall and another said that her mother had always been scared of the ghost when working in The White Lion. That one was said to be the ghost of a lady, possibly with two child ghosts with her.

One person recalled being told that when one particular house in Hadleigh was being renovated, they came across two mummified cats in the wall. When the floor was pulled up to be repaired and replaced, they found a hag stone and part of a James the 1st Bible. The mummified cats were there to keep witches out, and the hag stone and bible extract were thought to be indicative that an exorcism had taken place there. A hagstone is a rock which has a naturally occurring hole worn through the centre of it – usually as a result of water erosion. They are believed to have occult properties in many older religions around the world.

One lady who lived on the High Street for four years said there was always something strange around the fireplace of their old cottage. Acorns were often to be heard dropping down the chimney and bouncing off the little ornaments which sat on the hearth. Sometimes the acorns would seem to drop elsewhere in the room as if out of thin air. Since the property was on the High Street, where there are no trees nearby which could be shedding their produce, or harbouring squirrels who could otherwise have perhaps been the culprits. The family always assumed it was the spirit of their cat who had been knocked down by a car, but who had loved playing with acorns when alive: knocking them around as if they were little footballs.

Apparently in another of the properties, the residents got so fed up with "someone" peeking through their dining room door at them as they sat in the living room that they put up a curtain so that they couldn't see the ghost anymore!

The Town Hall ghost was seen in about 1986 when the witness involved was working in the bar at the top of the town hall. She was cleaning up after closing when she heard footsteps coming up behind her while she was busy putting glasses away. She glanced behind her and saw a lady with blonde hair and a headscarf on standing at the bar. She assumed it was her colleague who was also working that night, so just casually told her that she wouldn't be long and would be down in a minute. When she finished she went downstairs, but was told that her friend had actually left some time earlier – when the bar was not yet closed.

HARPENDEN, Hertfordshire

I came across a source story which said that there was an old terraced cottage behind the Silver Cup pub in Harpenden which was haunted by a soldier.

When I asked locally, the lady whose cottage it was contacted me and told me about the apparition as a first-hand account. She explained that she used to live there in the 1960s with her young son, who would regularly see the spirit of a soldier wearing a First World War uniform in the house. Her story had made the local press at the time, so she thinks that was probably the origin of the version of events which I had found. She no longer lives locally, so although she was able to supply the actual address, she did not know whether the haunting had continued in the years since she had left the property.

Other locals mentioned a now demolished house called Hazelbank in the vicinity, but further along the same stretch of road, which was abandoned and derelict. Not surprisingly, and in the way empty old buildings often do, for a while that gained a reputation as a haunted house. Some local residents remember that in the 1980s teenagers used to dare each other to visit the abandoned old building and would creep each other out with their stories.

As one correspondent explained, "In the late 70's, early 80's it had been derelict for many years and was fenced off by high wooden boards as well as being shielded by overgrown bushes of the garden." She described how the fact that it was empty and boarded to prevent entry just added an aura of intrigue and an element of fear to the young children of the area, who of course could still access the house through holes in the fencing that only children could get through.

As she stated, "The forbidden area was a natural pull to us children with wild imaginations that craved adventures, so it was no surprise that before long it had been dubbed as haunted with many wild stories circulating as to the reasons why this large house hidden away from us all had come to be abandoned and left undisturbed for so many years...

"We all speculated on the reasons and they became more and more embellished with gruesome stories of what may have occurred. The stories were all centred on the premise that a member of that family who had lived there had gone on a murder spree, taking the lives of all their family members. The tales told how the culprit was never caught by the authorities, and had been able to carry on living undetected in the decaying old house because of the many secret rooms and passageways only he had knowledge of."

She explained that there were rooms in that house that were closed off and secret doorways that led into the walls that could take you from one part of the house into another. The rooms on the top floor were part of the attic, and it was possible to walk around the entire floor by entering into the space beneath the eaves that surrounded it. As children exploring, they found that some parts of the staircases had decayed and rotted away, so that they were inaccessible and blocked off. Despite these hazards, over time the children found the other secret ways to get from one part of the house to another.

As she said, "There were still items of furniture in some rooms that were covered in dust and cobwebs so that decay and sense of abandonment added to the notion of it being a deserted house that must be haunted. With our imaginations already running wild, any noise that was more likely from the wildlife such as mice, rats and birds that had made their homes there was enough to send us into sheer panic and have us running for the way out of there as quickly as possible totally convinced that what we had heard was either the ghosts of the dead who were slaughtered there or the sounds of the murderer who lived in the cavities of the walls coming for us."

It remained a favourite playground of the local children for some time, who were forever daring one another to enter its spooky depths, but out of all of those visits there never seems to have been any actual "real" ghostly encounters.

One lady said that her house in The Spinney, further north in the small town, was haunted. As they were interested in finding out more about their resident ghost, they had held a séance, during which they had discovered that his name was John Long. They believed that he had been living with someone but was not married, and had been hanged for crimes unknown. He haunted the land now occupied by the house, rather than the building itself.

HAWKHURST, Kent

One gentleman told me about his family farm, close to the ancient town of Hawkhurst in Kent - a settlement which can claim at least a thousand years of history.

His family were originally French, and fled to England to land they owned there to escape the French Revolution in 1848. My correspondent had been born in 1948 at their family home, which was a very ancient farm house which had been in their family for at least the intervening century since they fled from the war.

From a very young age, he was aware of the family tradition that their farmhouse and surrounding gardens were haunted by the ghost of what was always described as a very beautiful lady.

She was frequently seen leaving the farmhouse, wearing a full length gown made of beautifully delicate flowing lace, and would walk out of the garden and across the lane to the old ale house opposite which at that time still brewed its own beer.

His own mother, a very well educated lady, had joined the army to "do her bit" for the country at the start of the Second World War, and had followed the invasion forces across Europe all the way to Dresden, carrying out her duties in Administration to the very best of her abilities in difficult circumstances, and helping defeated German families to try and reunite and start the process of rebuilding.

She returned to the UK two years after the war ended, and married our correspondent's father, settling down to life on the family farm. Apparently, she became accustomed to seeing the Beautiful Lady, and over time accepted that ghosts were in fact a real and present part of everyday life.

My correspondent told me how in 1972 his Aunt, who was his mother's younger sister, came to stay with the family for an extended visit to give birth to her third child, since her husband was away on a ten year contract running a mineral mine in a very remote area in Australia. It was felt to be a better idea for her to stay and have the support of family around her during the days of the birth and after, rather than struggle alone.

The Aunt was settled into a comfortable, well-appointed bedroom which afforded her a lovely view of the garden, and of the lane beyond. It also gave her a lovely view of the Beautiful Lady ghost, whom she remarked upon as seeing walk the garden almost every day during her own confinement.

Eventually, time marched on and my correspondent's parents died, and the farmhouse itself was sold. Although he has continued to live in one of the farm cottages across the lane from the main house for another 42 years, neither he nor any of the family have seen the Beautiful Lady ghost again since the house was sold.

HITCHIN, Hertfordshire – RICHARD REASON PIANOS

I was contacted by a gentleman who used to work at a Richard Reason Pianos in Hitchin. He explained that the shop was well known for its haunting, and had been visited by paranormal research teams.

The building has housed the Piano shop since the 1970s, but prior to then had been a builders merchant for probably a couple of hundred years. Parts of the property actually date back to the 1500s.

My correspondent said that he had worked there for around 20 years, and had a few experiences himself in that time. He was working busily one particular day, when a shadowy male figure walked past him, making that whole side of his body go cold as it passed.

On another occasion, whilst alone in the shop, he saw a lady in what looked to him to be Victorian style attire, walk slowly around the shop as if looking at the items on display. Since that first time, he has glimpsed her on several more occasions.

On another normal working day, he reached for something on a shelf - only to find his arm inexplicably blocked as if there were something invisible standing between him and the shelf!

He stopped working at the shop in 2013, but when he visited a few months back in 2019 to pick up some parts, he had the distinct feeling of someone putting their arm around his shoulders. I wonder if the ghosts were glad to see him back!

I wrote to the owner of the shop, who confirmed that quite a few people had agreed the shop was haunted, but he himself has been there for all these years and never seen or sensed anything.

HORLEY - Surrey - HORLEY ROW

A lady wrote to me to tell me that she used to live, many years ago, in a house on Horley Row in Horley, Surrey. The house itself was partially knocked down in later years in order to put in an access road to the car park of The Chequers Hotel. In the years since that renovation, the hotel itself has now fallen into disuse and stands empty, slowly crumbling and succumbing to vandalism.

My witness remembered that they had the ghost of a Victorian lady who frequented their home, and who had a particular penchant for wanting to open their linen cupboard during the night! The linen cupboard was at that time kept securely locked, and later on they took to screwing it shut to try and thwart the insistent ghost.

Her mother was the one who actually saw the apparition, on several occasions, and that was how they knew it was a lady in Victorian dress who was messing about with the cupboard.

After the family moved out, and before the property was partially demolished, it spent some time as a Bed & Breakfast establishment which lorry drivers often used, since it lay so conveniently next to the main A23. My correspondent remembers being told how five lorry drivers staying there one night all rushed out of the building in a high state of agitation after meeting the ghost.

HOUGHTON REGIS, Bedfordshire – TAVISTOCK PLACE

A gentleman told me that a few years ago, he and his family lived at a property which was a Victorian era cottage in Tavistock Place in Houghton Regis. He described the location as being at the end of Drury Lane, but I have struggled to locate it. They suspected for some time that the place was haunted, as they would inexplicably encounter the smell of burning in the house at odd times, when there was nothing to account for it.

Eventually, they invited a clairvoyant round to the house, who told them that there had once been a fire in the property and that someone had burned to death there.

Sometime after that, they took an old carpet up in one of the rooms and found some beautiful old quarry tiles underneath. They were at first planning to leave the lovely old floor showing, except for the fact that in one area there was a black mark as of burning. They tried cleaning them but every time, the mark would soon show back through again a few days later. Eventually they admitted defeat and laid a wooden floor over the attractive, but seemingly haunted, old tiles.

HUNNINGHAM, Warwickshire

My witness Jake, who appeared earlier in this book, worked at the picturesque riverside pub The Red Lion until 2003, earning extra cash whilst studying.

He recalled that at the time, the owners lived upstairs and although they were sceptical about anything paranormal, they admitted that something about the place did puzzle them. They owned two beautiful Doberman dogs – not normally known as a fainthearted breed! They said that they were unable to explain why their dogs would often stare at a particular piece of blank wall in the flat upstairs and bark at it, which was not usual behaviour for them.

Jake also remembered that on one occasion the ghost of a child, but with no legs visible, was seen in the upstairs area.

IPSWICH, Suffolk – THE ANCIENT HOUSE

The Ancient House is an astonishing looking building on the Buttermarket in Ipswich. It has an ornately carved frontage, with overhanging upper storeys, and curved upper bay windows. Engraved on the front in bright heraldic colours is the Royal Coat of Arms "Dieu et mon droit". It is a Grade I listed building dating from the 1400s, and is sometimes also referred to as Sparrowe's House after a former owner.

It is currently a shop, housing the business "Lakeland", who sell kitchenware, innovative gadgets, and cooking utensils. The building itself has long been rumoured to have a ghost, and it is said that things move about in the shop sometimes. In 1997, staff of the store experienced a series of strange happenings with flowers being inexplicably rearranged, and a staff member getting locked in the cellar until the door suddenly burst open without aid.

When I asked locally if anyone knew anything of the ghost, I got some interesting responses.

Three people said they had never experienced anything there. One lady said the property was definitely not haunted, but that the tea shop nearby in St Stephens Lane is, as is a tomb embedded in the wall of St Stephen's church.

Two people said they **had** felt something whilst visiting. One lady described it as just a feeling that "something" was present. Another said it was in one of the rooms upstairs that she felt a presence, and that she had been told Charles Dickens once visited the property.

One lady said that she worked there for her first job, as an office junior, in the 1970s. She said that she herself never experienced anything paranormal, but the statue of King Charles which was kept up in the attic rooms at that time used to give her the creeps. She had also heard some of the older employees chatting about the haunting and they were sure it was real.

One lady recalled that the original legend she was told was that there was once a married couple living in the house – many long years ago, whose surname happened also to be Lakeland, although with no relation to the current shop name. Apparently the couple had a contretemps in the street outside their house one day, and the wife Mary was heard to scream at her husband in a fit of rage, "I wish you were dead!" Unfortunately for her, the husband did in fact die a few days later, and so the good townspeople decided that Mary must in fact be a witch, and took her up to Rushmere Heath to be burned at the stake.

A little digging shows that Matthew Hopkins, the Witchfinder General, did in fact try in court and then convict a Mary Lakeland of witchcraft in Ipswich, and had her burned at the stake on Tuesday 9th September 1645. She was the wife of the town Barber, and was said to have admitted murdering her husband. In addition, she confessed to causing the death of a man who could not repay a loan she had made him, and murdering the maid of one Mrs Jennings, who had sent the poor hapless maid to Mary to ask for the repayment of a loan Mrs Jennings had made. She also admitted to sinking a ship, and causing a man to suffer a wasting illness, after making a pact with the Devil and his demons.

Contrary to popular belief, it was actually very rare for witches to be burned at the stake, but since Mary was being convicted of murder, her crime came under the punishment rules for petty-treason.

KENILWORTH, Warwickshire – REDFERN AVENUE

The original source story I found for Redfern Avenue said that in 1978 a Mrs Valerie Graham started hearing the sound of monks chanting during the middle of the night. The sound was always most audible from the back of the house she lived in, and was definitely coming from outside. Her husband was a heavy sleeper, and never woke up in time to hear it.

Then one day, she heard the sound during the middle of the afternoon – but was astonished to find that her husband, although now of course wide awake, still couldn't hear it. She might have been left thinking she was hearing things, except she found out that someone else further down the road had also been hearing it.

When I asked locally whether anyone had heard anything, I got some interesting responses. I never say, when going out looking for fresh evidence, exactly what my source evidence was or what the haunting is meant to manifest itself as. I just ask whether people are aware of a haunting and can tell me of their own experiences. This is because, of course, I don't want to contaminate any responses with a preconceived notion of what they should be looking for, and neither do I want to prevent anyone coming forward because what they experienced in the locale I'm interested in didn't "fit the profile" of what I was asking about.

Two people casually answered that yes, of course all the roads around there are haunted, and one told me that she has seen the apparitions of children wearing Victorian style clothing walking down the Avenue. On other occasions, she has seen men in white shirts standing in the windows of the houses looking out.

One lady mentioned that in her Mum's house she has heard male voices saying her name, and on one occasion the hot tap suddenly turned on full blast in front of her. She has also had glasses mysteriously smash when no-one was near them.

On the other hand, several people answered who said that they had never heard of anything unusual in the Avenue, even though at least one of them had lived there for over forty years.

And yet, one lady came forward to say that a friend of hers, who really didn't believe in anything supernatural, had once heard the sound of monks chanting down this road.

Curiously, the houses there today are pretty modern, terraced houses on a normal suburban housing estate. The original source story related the possible haunting to the nearby Abbeyfields, site of the Kenilworth Priory: but actually Redfern Avenue doesn't really seem close enough to that to necessarily be linked.

One lady told me that the story she had heard was that around the end of August or beginning of September each year, people would sometimes hear the sound of a woman begging for help in the wee small hours of the morning. However, if they try to investigate the sounds by going outside, the noise instantly stops. She said that the tale she had heard was that a lady was attacked and robbed along there sometime in the 18th century, and during the attack her baby daughter was struck and killed. The sound of the crying is said to be her spirit returning to the site and begging for the life of her poor innocent baby daughter to be spared.

My witness had herself had heard the sound many years ago, and remembered that when she heard the sound, she had felt very unsettled by it, even though she had not at first realised she was listening to anything supernatural. It had started quite abruptly, and had made her jump because at first the sound seemed to be literally right behind her. The thing that that had unsettled her was that the sound itself seemed to come from different directions, depending on how she tilted her head around trying to locate it as she walked. There was no wind that day to be carrying the sound, and the area was very quiet.

She realised that what she had been hearing was not natural (even though she had been trying in vain to tell herself it must just be an animal or something) when she reached her friend's house, which she was walking to, and told them about the sound. Her friend explained that the ghost was known locally as The Red Girl and was a sound that they had frequently heard.

Several people mentioned that there were rumours of ghosts in nearby Webster Avenue, just the other side of the railway track, because there used to be a convalescent home there run by nuns.

Interestingly, one person mentioned that Abbeyfields was supposed to have the spirit of the Red Monk walking through it - so one can't help but wonder whether the story of the Red Girl and the Red Monk have somehow become mixed up over the years?

I was also told that a property in Sunshine Close, (mostly modern chalet style bungalows) further south in Kenilworth, was haunted in 1984 by a ghost wearing a maid's uniform complete with mob cap.

KILMACOLM, Scotland – THE HYDRO HOTEL

The Old Hydro Hotel was a magnificent looking building, where only the very wealthy could afford to stay in its luxurious rooms and take their leisure on its private golf course. It succumbed to the changing times over the years however, and was eventually demolished having stood in ruins for a while. It stood somewhere near the West Glen Road, and the housing estate now there was built over the site.

One witness told me that about 30 years or so ago, her (then) husband took a photograph of the old abandoned building. When he had the picture developed, there was clearly a face to be seen in one of the upstairs windows.

Several other people had heard of a ghost at The Hydro, and one identified it as having been known as The White Lady. Some remembered playing around the ruins as children and hunting for the ghost.

Whilst trying to find out exactly where The Hydro stood, I did come across a little gem. This was from 1953 and was written about a time some fifty years earlier than that - so the events would have been at the turn of the century in around 1903 or so:

"Memories of Kilmacolm
A talk given by Brown McMinn Esq. in Old St. Columba Hall
on the evening of Tuesday, 9th February, 1953"

In his talk, the gentleman explained that in those days, they all had a firm belief in ghosts, and most boys thought they had seen one on at least one or two occasions.

He described how there was a legend in the village of Kilmacolm at the time that there had been a drowning accident when The Hydro was being built. One of the workmen had walked down into the village one evening and had partaken of a few too many drinks - resulting in him missing his footing as he crossed the little bridge which spanned the burn halfway up Glenmosston, falling into the churning waters below, and drowning.

He remembered that one lad who had the job of delivering milk up in that area, claimed that on two successive nights he had been chased by the ghost of the drowned man, right down to the gate of The Hydro below Kilmory.

On the third evening, he gathered together a little band of his mates, and they bravely armed themselves with large stones to throw at the ghost. At first, nothing happened, and each boy began to bravely brag of what he would have done had the ghose shown itself. Suddenly, they became aware of the ominous sound of footfalls behind them, and turning around, saw the ghost coming straight for them out of the dark. Running for their lives, they were relieved when the "ghost" turned into the gates of the Hydro - it was actually a well-known athlete out training for his running...

One gentleman remarked that his parents in law had lived along nearby Bridge of Weir Road in the 1960s, and their house was haunted by a ghost who would move things around.

KNOWLTON, Dorset - KNOWLTON CHURCH AND EARTHWORKS

This is a very picturesque site, with the hollowed out shell of the ruined church standing as it does in the centre of the remains of a Neolithic earthwork. Built in the 12th century on top of the older, probably pagan site, it was clearly one of the attempts by the "new" religion Christianity to oust its predecessors.

The church was at one time surrounded by a thriving community, but the local inhabitants were decimated by the arrival of the Black Death in the 1500s. Although the population dwindled dramatically, with buildings abandoned and the church eventually left standing on its own, it continued to remain in service until the 1700s, when its roof finally collapsed and its slow crumble into dust began in earnest.

Interestingly, the very fabric of the walls are thought to contain some of the broken up remains of standing stones that would have been located at the site originally.

It is said to be the haunt of a ghostly horse and rider who cross the site in the middle of the night – riding through the church as if it simply didn't exist. This would suggest a much older ghost – maybe even one of the Neolithic men to whom the site would have held great significance.

Supposedly, a face has been seen peering from the top window of the tower, and the figure of a woman has been seen kneeling on the ground outside the church – apparently weeping.

The site is often visited by paranormal groups, who have reported disembodied voices.

One lady wrote to me to tell me what she knows of the ghosts around this beautiful old ruined church. She said that the very first time she visited the ruin, she heard the distinct sound of a baby crying. A medium who was visiting with them said that this was related to the ghost of a young woman who, when pregnant, was either pushed or jumped from the tower of the church.

She said that often people have detected the distinct smell of hay and horses around the site, even though it sits so isolated. She told me that sometimes the site seems quite benevolent, but other times the atmosphere will turn very heavy and foreboding. Some paranormal teams investigating at the site have found strange areas of pitch black where even the natural ambient light seems to dim at night. They have also recorded that sometimes EMF (Electro-magnetic Field) meters show readings which are practically off the scale.

LITTLECOTE MANOR, Wiltshire

Littlecote House is now a very attractive hotel in Wiltshire, not far from Hungerford. Originally a medieval mansion, it was inhabited by the de Calstone family from around 1290, and the Tudor mansion which replaced the original building was built sometime after 1490. King Henry VIII is said to have courted Jane Seymour at the house.

In 1592 its conversion to the Elizabethan brick mansion seen today was completed by its then owner Sir John Popham. It boasts that as well as King Henry VIII, James I, Charles II, and William of Orange have all stayed there.

During the Second World War the house was the headquarters of 34th Army Tank Brigade, commanded by Brigadier J Noel Tetley. In 1996 it was bought and converted into the hotel which it is today.

It has long been rumoured to house several ghosts, which is perhaps not surprising given its long and colourful history. There is supposed to be the spectre of a black dog on the staircase, who seems quite real until you attempt to pet him - when his non corporeal nature becomes apparent.

There is also the ghost of former owner "Wild Will Darrell" who died when thrown from his horse, and also by a mother screaming for her baby, who was apparently thrown onto the fire by Wild Will in a fit of temper. Apparently in 1970 a visitor to the house saw a ghostly lady carrying a child in the haunted bedroom where the murder happened. The ghost is often seen wearing blue, and sometimes the sound of a crying baby can be heard from the room.

One correspondent told me that her father and his pals, when very much younger, once camped out all night in the grounds of the lovely old Hall - hoping to see the headless figure of Wild Will on his horse. Unfortunately their vigil did not pay off.

Her grandfather, however, was once driving past Littlecote Manor, travelling from Aldbourne to Chilton Foliat along the B4192. Suddenly, a man wearing very old fashioned clothes stepped out into the road right in front of his car. At that time, there were often groups in the area doing "historic re-enactments", and so it was not entirely uncommon to see people in very outdated garb walking around. Both her grandfather and a driver passing the other way stopped their cars and got out to look however, because of how close to the car the figure had stepped out - making both drivers fear he must have been struck.

Despite their best efforts searching the immediate vicinity, it was quickly clear that there was no sign of anyone living having stepped into the road..

Her grandfather had needed a stiff whisky when he finally made it to his destination.

Apparently, one of my correspondents school friends also used to say that her grandmother worked at the Hall, and would regale the family with the latest story of things that the other staff working there had witnessed which were not "of this world".

LITTLE WALSINGHAM, Norfolk

One correspondent wrote to me to tell me of her time living in a Grade II listed property not far from Holkham Hall in Little Walsingham. The house was probably originally two separate dwellings which have long since been redesigned into one - and moreover, the roof trusses apparently show there is a possibility of there originally having been three properties.

My correspondent and her family bought the house some years ago, and on her first night staying there she chose one of the oldest rooms in the buildings, which still had some of the original wall paintings showing.

As she dozed off, tired after her busy day, she rather disturbingly became aware of a sensation of several people standing in the room just looking at her. After a few moments the sensation faded away, and she was happy to report they never made a reappearance - so she presumed they decided in favour of her staying!

She said that the most active room in the house was the old Dining Hall. It had a massive beamed fireplace complete with apertures used as bread ovens. She explained, "Whenever I formally set the dining table for a dinner party I would be aware of two people approaching the table and standing just beside it, one behind the other." Usually, she could never see anything, just sense the presence.

However, an evening came where they had a friend staying with them who was a member of the Dutch Navy, and normally quite a stoic person with no truck for nonsense or flights of fancy. Nevertheless, on this evening as the table was being laid, both my correspondent and her guest caught a glimpse of the two extra visitors: one was a lady wearing a voluminous red skirt, with a white ruff around her neck and a neat black bolero style jacket, standing with her hands folded neatly in front of her.

The other was a tall gentleman, standing slightly in front of his lady companion, who wore black knee breeches, black stockings, and pointed shoes. He had a white high necked ruffled collar, and longish hair peeking out from under his hat. They stood there for a moment before fading from sight to the astonishment of our witness and her guest. Throughout the rest of the Navy Officer's stay, from time to time their presence would be felt again, but they never appeared as clearly as they had on that first occasion.

A local historian told her that the well in the garden had a reputation of having been used to toss suspected witches into, and this always made her feel quite creeped out by its presence. Personally - I find this to be a strange concept - and probably not true. Why on earth would a busy and well-appointed house with its own well allow its water supply to be poisoned and rendered useless in this way?

LOUTH, Lincolnshire – EASTFIELD STREET

A gentleman wrote to me to tell me about the house he grew up in, which was in Louth in Lincolnshire. The property was on the east side of the town, on Eastfield Road, and it was during the 1980s when he was growing up there that things would happen.

He explained that most of the occurrences seemed to be during the winter months, when the nights had drawn in and dark would come early. On those evenings, as the family sat down to eat their evening meal, they would hear someone walk down the passage at the side of the house. A moment later a shadow would pass the window, and then the back door would open by itself - just as if someone had just returned home and casually walked in.

He said that it was particularly odd because that back door was always a bit of a problem - because in the damp winter months it would noticeably swell and be inclined to stick, so that opening it usually meant giving it quite a hefty kick. And yet whatever opened it on these dark nights seemed able to do so with no problem at all.

He explained that this normally happened between 6pm and 7pm in the evening, and since the house itself sat on the site of what was once a pub serving the busy Louth canal trade, the family fell into the habit of remarking "it must be opening time!" and carrying on with their meal after shutting the door to keep the cold winter air out.

He told me that his brother once reported seeing what he described as Roman soldiers march through their front room - but he was on his own at the time and no-one else ever witnessed that, so he felt that he was unable to corroborate that.

LOUTH, Lincolnshire – JAMES STREET

The same witness also recounted to me a tale which his own father, now sadly deceased, used to like to repeat for the family. His father worked as a skilled joiner for a local company based in James Street. He and his work mates were once sent out to do some work on an older property on the outskirts of the town - possibly an old rectory or something similar.

They were all working away busily one day, when the property owner came by and told them they would have to carry on working unsupervised, since he was going into town to run an errand. The men were not perturbed - they all knew their work well and carried on industriously.

In due course, lunchtime rolled around and the men thankfully stopped their work to take a break. The owner still hadn't returned, so perhaps feeling a little braver than they would have done, they decided to have a proper sit down in a room which housed a piano. One of the men - perhaps a little too cheekily - thought he might have a little tinkle on the piano keys. However, as his fingers touched the musical instrument, it immediately became apparent that it was precariously balanced, supported by a tin with some sort of treacle like substance in it. To their horror, this tin was inadvertently tipped over, and the oozing mess fell out across the hardwood floor. Everyone scrambled to their knees to clean it up before it had a chance to stain, but to their horror, they heard the front door open and the approaching sound of footsteps down the hallway.

Certain they were about to be caught out in their misbehaviour by the owner of the house returning, they waited in mute misery for the door to the room to open and the inevitable recriminations from an angry house owner to begin. After a few moments, nothing had happened, and nothing further was heard, so they plucked up the courage to face the consequences and opened the door to go and speak to the owner.

There was no-one there, and no-one had come home. They were still alone in the property.

His father would always say that although they got the mess cleaned up and no harm done, the sound of those disembodied footsteps had quite a profound effect for some time after on all of the men who were there that day, as they all so clearly heard it.

LOUTH, Lincolnshire – VARIOUS

Another gentleman wrote to me to tell me of his own experience as a young lad in the 1950's. His family at the time lived in Commercial Road, prior to moving out in 1956. He explained that they would experience doors opening by themselves and the sound of footsteps going down the stairs in the middle of the night.

At the time, as a young boy himself, he was going through a period of sleepwalking, so at first when they heard the sounds the parents would think it was their son having one of his episodes, and the father would calmly follow the footsteps out through the opened front door, expecting to find his son and take him back to his bed. However, they would find this was not their lad at all – he was still sound asleep and safely tucked up in bed.

On some occasions, they distinctly heard what they identified as the sound of a cobbler tapping away on the shoes he was busy mending. Curiously, many years later his Aunt, who lived elsewhere in the town and took in police cadets as lodgers, told them that one of her "lads" was on a night patrol down Commercial Rd when he saw a small man with a beard and wearing a leather pinafore in the road in front of him. Approaching the man to ask what he was doing out so late, he was horrified when the figure just disappeared right in front of his eyes. He refused to ever patrol that street alone again.

One gentleman told me that he used to live in one of the houses in St Marys Road, in Westor, an area of Louth. He believed that the properties had been built over the remains of an old monastery, and told me that everyone who lived along there reported strange things happening in their houses.

He told me that in their house, they would often hear the sound of deep, heavy breathing – when you knew you were alone in the house..

Another witness wrote to tell me that she had worked at the pub known as The Cellars in Louth for many years. She said that there were a few strange happenings over the years, but the one which really stood out for her was the night she saw a full figured apparition.

It was very late in the evening, and the staff had started cleaning up ready to close for the night, whilst the last few stragglers drank up, bade their good nights, and made their way out of the door.

She noticed one man, whom she described as wearing a grey jumper and jeans, but looking a bit old fashioned, as if he was dressed in 1950s era clothing, walk past her and turn into the Ladies' toilet area.

She immediately stopped what she was doing and followed him in, intending to point out his error and redirect him into the Gents before he startled any lady customers who might be using the facilities before making their way home. She was literally a moment behind him as she walked into the bathroom calling out to him - only to find the room completely empty.

Rick, a retired policeman, wrote in to say that he remembered a crew of policemen coming in one night literally as white as sheets - they had just seen the ghost of the Green Lady float across the road in front of their patrol car outside Thorpe Hall. She had drifted through the beam of their headlights at about 3am on the cold night and made her way into Deighton Close - turning to look solemnly at their car as she passed. She was literally floating - she appeared to have no legs below the knee...

Apparently the normally tough and pragmatic policeman were in quite a state of shock about what they had just seen, and were subdued and pale. It took ages in the warmth and light of the police station for them to calm down and return to some sort of normal state of mind.

I did have to have a little chuckle to myself at one person who responded though. They just typed, "Ghosts.....Deep Sigh." I liked the meaningful pause and implied exasperated scepticism in the simple words.

A gentleman told me that Boyes Department store on Mercer Row is also haunted – by the ghost of a young girl who apparently, so legend has it, drowned in a well.

He worked there for a time from 2007 to 2009, and one particular day he was on the very top floor walking towards the lift. A girl was walking towards him, and he thought she was one of the other staff who worked there, and greeted her as they passed one another in the corridor. A moment later he stepped up to the lift, just as it stopped at his floor and the doors opened. Out stepped the member of staff he thought he had just passed and greeted in the corridor. So who was the girl he had actually greeted?

At the time, he lived in a flat above one of the neighbouring shops, and one evening he saw the same girl walk past the bottom of the stairs which led into his building and up to the shop door. The next day at work, he and his colleague checked the CCTV footage of the store, because he was curious as to who it was he had now seen twice.

He knew for sure then that what he was seeing was not part of the mundane everyday world, because at the precise time he had seen her walking up to the store door, the CCTV footage showed absolutely no sign of anyone there..

Other correspondents also mentioned that there are many other ghost stories to be explored around Louth: There is said to be a ghost girl at Kelstern Crossroads on the road from Louth to Ludford, a ghostly horse outside Caedby, and the ghost of a lady who fell from her horse and broke her neck on Breakneck Lane, to name but a few..

LUDLOW, Shropshire – CASTLE LODGE

Castle Lodge in Ludlow is an astonishing medieval building in the heart of the town. Currently under new ownership, it looks like it might be getting a makeover to become a feature boutique cafe and hotel.

Rebuilt in 1580 to the glorious building we see today, it has had a long history of suspected haunting. There is supposedly the ghost of a teenage girl wearing Tudor costume, who is seen walking the attic corridors and the nursery. Legend has it that this is the ghost of Catherine of Aragon, who later became one of King Henry VIII's wives, returning to a site where she once was happy. There is one account of a young man fleeing from the upper floor after he encountered her ghost and saw her walk through a closed door.

Curiously, one gentleman told me that his step-grandfather once made a dolls house replica of the building - perhaps twenty years ago or so. I wonder where that is now, as apparently the family sold it.

One lady told me that her uncle had lived in the Lodge sometime in the mid 1920's into the early 1930's, but never experienced anything supernatural during his time there.

Another lady told me that a few years ago, she and her family visited the property, which was a museum at that time, for a day out. It was February half term, and the weather was cold and frosty, so she was looking for something entertaining to do with her children who were then aged 8 and 11 years old. She said it felt strange from the moment they walked in. Although fires had been lit to warm the place, despite their warmth and light, the place somehow still had a dull and lifeless feel to it which made for quite an oppressive atmosphere.

As they made their way upstairs, she felt increasingly uneasy and the oppressive atmosphere was starting to make her feel physically queasy, but she did not say anything to the children. They were the only people visiting, and she certainly didn't want to spoil the day out. However, as they started to look round the upper floor, her son started to shiver, and complained that he didn't like it up there.

They were standing in a bedroom at the front of the house, and for just a second she was sure she heard voices in the nearby child's room, even though she knew no other living person was there. She still did not say anything to the children, but by now both of them were complaining that they didn't like it there, so she decided to call it quits and they left. She said that despite the cold day outside, the family actually immediately felt better and even warmer the moment they left the building.

MALMESBURY, Wiltshire – BURTON HILL

There is an area on the outskirts of the beautiful and atmospheric old town of Malmesbury called Burton Hill. There is a hospital in the area, and also the wonderful old building which until 2007 was the Burton Hill School. I originally wrote about this locale in my third book, The Roadmap of British Ghosts, because the road itself here, the A429, is said to be haunted.

However, a lot of information came forward about the buildings themselves, so for completeness I am writing about it again and updating the information. Originally, I mentioned the dark figure often seen on the road along here, and also the spectre of a coach and horses which had originally crashed into a pool along there. One lady had come forward then to say it was actually an ancestor of hers who was killed in that coach crash.

Other people also mentioned the time they worked in the hospital. One lady said that they had a ghost of a grey lady who would walk down the hospital corridors, and many of the nursing staff were really reluctant to go up into the attic areas to get changed out of their uniforms before going home. She said the rooms up there always seemed creepy with a cold feeling about them. Another lady came forward to verify the account, saying she had an office which faced onto the corridor and would sometimes glimpse the Grey Lady walking along outside her office. She said the spectre would appear as quite a solid figure, but more shadow than with actual defined features. She had been told that the ghost was that of a matron who had died in a fire, and that her own office now occupied the site of what had once been the matron's living quarters.

On one occasion, two colleagues were making themselves a well-earned cup of tea in the little kitchenette when they heard the heavy main door open and someone started to walk along the corridor. They looked out of the kitchen, wondering who it was since the door was operated by keypad only and they weren't expecting anyone, only to see the Grey Lady walk by and disappear into one of the offices.

A gentleman told me that his paternal grandfather and father used to live at Burton Hill when his father was himself a child. His grandfather had the duty of keeping an eye on The Priory whenever the then owners were away, and used to complain that oftimes, he would go in and check the place over, carefully lock up and switch off all the lights, then walk outside and find some of the lights had been mysteriously switched back on.

Another lady told me that when working the night shift at what was then the residential school, she saw the Grey Lady ghost. And another correspondent said that her father had once been the Deputy Head of the school and told her that the ghost of the grey lady mostly frequented the first floor room which overlooked the garden, but was also sometimes seen walking in the garden as well.

MANBY AIRFIELD, Lincolnshire

Interestingly, a retired Police officer, Rick, wrote to me to tell me about his experience, which had left a lasting impression. He and his crew partner were out in their patrol car, on a very cold November night a few years ago, possibly around 1997. It was a horrible foggy night, so they had parked their vehicle up near the top end of Manby Airfield, not far from the Control tower.

At around 2am, they suddenly became aware of a low rumbling noise coming from the direction the car was pointed.

His colleague asked, "What the hell is that?" and they both peered into the fog. Rick replied that he thought it sounded like a Lancaster. They listened in astonishment to the sound of the loud engines taxiing along the runway in front of their car, passing to their left. They could clearly hear it make the turn onto the runway and start to rev its engines up as if for take-off. They started their car up and followed the sound – but at no point was there anything to be seen. And almost as suddenly as it had started, the sound faded into the night – but not in the way of a plane taking off and leaving – just in the way of a static sound dying away. Although they searched around for a while longer, they could not find any other planes active on the runway, nor any explanation for what they had just heard.

Rick is certain it was the sound of a Lancaster he was following and has no explanation for what happened. Lancasters are very rare planes to still be flying today (worldwide there are thought to be only two still airworthy!), and are very unlikely to be flying at 2am in the morning in thick fog.

His comment sparked the interest of someone else, who wrote to say he had checked it out, and Lancasters did in fact used to fly from that airfield. Apparently a number of other people have since told Rick that they too have heard the ghostly Lancaster, and some say the old Control Tower is definitely haunted.

A lady then told us that her mother used to work at the Nursing Home which was housed in a converted block on the old airbase at Manby Airfield. Her mother had told her about a night which had stayed in her memory, and was always adamant it was the truth.

She was working the night shift on this particular occasion in around 1990, and was tending to one of their residents in a downstairs room. She was on her own, chatting amiably to the old lady she was helping, but realised she needed the help of another nurse for a moment to help lift the patient into a better position to settle her. It was around 2am in the morning, and so for the most part, the building was very quiet with most of the residents sleeping peacefully.

She knew all the other care assistants were at that moment on the upper floor, as they had gone to answer one of the call bells which had sounded.

However, after a few moments of debating whether to go and call someone down, she heard the loud sound of footsteps coming down the corridor outside the room she was working in.

Relieved to think help was at hand, she called out for whoever it was to pop into the room and give help. The footsteps, however, never faltered but continued their measured tread past the doorway of the room she was in and on down the corridor. Assuming that whoever it was must not have heard her call out, she immediately popped her head out of the door to call them back.

Imagine her astonishment as she looked down a long empty corridor - with absolutely no sign of anyone walking away down it. It was only then that she realised that actually, the whole incident made no sense, because the footsteps had been the sound of booted feet on a tiled floor - and the corridor she was looking at was plushly carpeted. The last time it would have been tiled was when the airbase was still active.

Yet another lady came forward and told me that her late father had often told the story to the family of the ghost he saw whilst working at the airfield once. He used to work there in the 1960s, and part of his duties was to mow the grass.

He was mowing around a particular plane, and noticed underneath the fuselage that he could see that a man was standing on the other side of the aircraft - the legs of this other man were very plainly visible. However, as our witness pushed his mower around the nose of the plane and opened his mouth to greet whoever it was, he was astonished to find that no-one was there and no-one was anywhere near in sight.

He would also say that the mess hall and some of the other old buildings were known to be haunted - lights would turn on and off by themselves, and doors were known to open and close. He said the shenanigans would often frighten the living daylights out of the poor night time cleaning crew!

One witness said she worked at Manby in Tedder Hall in 2008, and although no smoking was allowed at that time, she would often smell cigar smoke in the corridor there. This prompted someone else to come forward to say that she still works there – and there is still sometimes the smell of cigar smoke where there should not be.

MARKYATE, Hertfordshire

A gentleman wrote to me to give me details of his experiences in the small Hertfordshire village of Markyate. It is a strangely elongated village, running as it does along a stretch of old Roman Road, and bypassed now by the more modern A5.

My correspondent lived for a while in the 1980s in the Vicarage which was at the top of the High Street. It is a relatively new build compared to other parts of the village, and sits next to the entrance to the lane leading up to the Graveyard.

He and his family moved in, and were settling in well with no problems. After a while, he was contacted by one of the previous incumbents, who after chatting for a while about more mundane routine matters, casually asked whether they had experienced anything from the ghost yet.

At that stage, they had not yet had any unusual happenings, so he was curious to know what his predecessor was referring to.

He was told that sometimes footsteps could be heard going up and down the staircase in the house. It was sometime later before they heard it for themselves, and when they finally did, they found that it was quite an innocuous sound which only happened every now and then, and was not in any way frightening to live with. They learned to just pretty much ignore it and accept it as part of the character of their new home.

He was also told by an older couple living in the village that their own house, also in the High Street, had a ghost. The husband told him how on one particular evening, he had fallen asleep whilst watching the television in their front room, without actually meaning to doze off. He had woken up with a start sometime later in the wee hours of the morning, to find that the television was still turned on but not showing any picture, as the broadcasts had long since finished and even the test card (which used to appear as a background picture with music playing once broadcasting finished for the day) had switched off.

In their lounge, they had an alcove in one corner of the room, and as the poor man awoke he realised that standing in it he could see the figure of a well-to-do lady in good quality clothing, which he thought might be from the 18th Century, wearing a large hat but completely motionless. The two regarded each other in solemn silence for a moment or two before she quietly faded away. Apparently he did not feel frightened - it was over too quickly for one thing, but also there was no sense of malice in the atmosphere.

My correspondent had also been told of a ghost which haunted Manor Farm just outside the village. He explained that, "The lady of the house at that time told me that once when her young nephew was staying with them, they put him in a bedroom at the top of the house to sleep.

"He came down to breakfast one morning and told her that he had woken up in the middle of the night to find that a lady was standing at the foot of his bed. He had not found her in the least bit frightening. He described her as wearing a simple rough dress made out of what appeared to be sacking, with a rope tied round her waist." Apparently the lady's husband had also seen the same apparition some years earlier when he was sleeping in the same room their nephew was now occupying.

MATFIELD, Kent - THE STAR PUB

Boasting a rather attractive outside seating patio area, The Star pub in this small Kentish village also apparently hosts some ghosts.

One lady told me that she was sitting with friends and her brother at the pub one evening, chatting and laughing and generally having a pleasant evening out. She herself was sitting with her back to the bar, so she didn't actually see what occurred - but the shocked reactions of her friends and their immediate recounting told her what she needed to know. Her brother explained that a pint of beer, almost full, had suddenly slid along the bar and crashed off the end of it, smashing itself on the floor below. Nobody was anywhere near it and nobody had touched it.

She explained that people in the pub said it was the spirit of a former landlord, who had a habit of showing his displeasure even from the afterlife when someone at "his" bar was talking about a subject he disagreed with.

The current tenant said he had heard many stories of the ghost in the pub over the years, and thought there was an old article in a newspaper about it dating back to the 1960s.

Another lady said that her own mother had been a barmaid at the pub for many years, and often used to recount the many strange goings on there were there. She thinks her mother might have featured in the newspaper article that had been mentioned by others.

MAYBOLE, Ayrshire – CROSSRAGUEL ABBEY

Crossraguel Abbey today is a fascinatingly picturesque ruined monument standing beside a small road in Ayrshire, Scotland. Properly named The Abbey of Saint Mary of Crossraguel, it is open for public viewing for a modest fee.

Much of the stonework is standing, and it forms a suitably atmospheric backdrop for the story of a ghostly monk that walks the ruins still, and also possibly a "Bogle" of a stone mason. A Bogle is a Scottish word for a ghost or supernatural being. There is a wonderfully preserved circular "Doocot" in the southwest corner of the Abbey - better known south of the Border as a Dovecot, and rumour also has it that there is a secret underground tunnel leading from here to nearby Baltersan Castle.

The ghost is said to be that of the Abbot of Crossraguel. He was captured by the fourth Earl of Cassillis, who took his prisoner to Culzean Castle and there roasted him over a fire until he gave in and signed the Abbey and its lands over to his tormentor.

Several people wrote to me about the monk of the Abbey, so it is clearly still a well-known legend in the area, although conversely a few people who had lived in the area most of their lives and even used to play in the ruins as children knew nothing of its reputation. One chap explained that one of his ancestors was named Baillie of Crossraguel in 1523.

One lady remembered hearing about the monk as a child, but also remembered tales of the ghost of a grey lady there too.

One person said that their friend's husband, normally a very sceptical, pragmatic and down to earth type of man, swears he saw the ghost of the monk whilst driving past the ruins one night.

Another lady wrote to tell me that she used to live in the tiny, whitewashed farmhouse just opposite the remains of the Abbey when she was around 10 years old: in around 2006. The family lived there until 2012.

At first, she was very happy living there despite its rather remote location in terms of immediate neighbours, but then she started having a series of recurring nightmares.

In every dream, there would be a sense of war going on, of fear and conflict, and each nightmare ended by her dying in the dream when a bomb fell on the house. The dreams seemed unusually dark for an otherwise normal ten-year old girl, but to be fair, as she says, they were learning about the World Wars in school at the time, and the house itself had a small metal bomb shelter built into the back garden.

She had a small sister who was around five years younger than herself, but just starting to really grasp full language and becoming a right little chatterbox, the way small children often are. One particular day, she was out in the garden playing by the swings, but curiously she was just pushing the empty swing rather than sitting on it herself, and chattering away to herself.

Her big sister tried to put her on the swing, thinking she perhaps wanted to have a go and have someone push her, but the little girl started crying instead and became very upset. She kept trying to tell her older sibling that "Robin" was sitting in the swing, and it was his turn to swing, not hers.

From then onwards, whenever something was broken or a wall got mysteriously drawn on by small hands with crayons, her sister would insist that Robin was just trying to get her into trouble. Very often, the older children in the house would catch a glimpse of someone rushing past behind them in the bathroom mirror, or would hear quiet voices talking in an adjoining room, but when they went in, no-one was there.

Upstairs, there was a long corridor with the bedrooms opening off it, and the children would hear the sound of feet running up and down it at night: and most creepily it would sometimes sound as if they were dragging their hands along the wall as they ran. Her own best friend would really try to avoid coming over to stay for the night, because she said that all the activity around this corridor and the bathroom "really freaked her out".

The activity would start around early evening time usually, and carry on right through until the early hours of the morning.

She never established whether there was a link between "Robin" and her own recurring dreams, but it does make you wonder.

MONMOUTH, Wales - OLD

COACH ROAD TOWARDS BAILEY PITT FARM

A gentleman wrote to me to tell me about his experience one autumn evening around dusk.

He is a keen runner, and likes to go for an evening run after the day's activities. This particular evening, he was running along Offa's Dyke Path just outside of Monmouth in Wales.

He suddenly realised, as he ran, that he could see something very odd on the lane which led down to the old Bailey's Pitt farm, which at that time was at least partially derelict.

He could see an orange luminescent glow moving along the lane – and watched it for about two minutes as he ran. It was about the size of an ordinary vehicle, but curiously he could clearly hear the sound of horses' hooves accompanying its movement. He said the hoof beats actually sounded like it was a team of horses moving at a swift pace. It eventually moved out of view, and left him feeling quite shaken as he knew that there is a legend that the path and lane are haunted by a spectral coach and horses.

NETTLEHAM, Lincolnshire

A correspondent from the Lincolnshire Paranormal Research Team wrote to me to tell me about a personal experience of hers.

She had been working her usual evening shift at a pub in around 1998, and was driving home alone at about midnight or so, travelling down the A46 between Nettleham and Welton. The road along here is fairly flat and level, bounded by a small hedge and occasional scrub trees for the most part, and with views across open, gently sloping or flat fields to either side. It was her usual route, and a road she was familiar with driving home down at night.

Suddenly, a brightly lit motorbike headlamp appeared in her rearview mirror. It was a little bit of a surprise, because the road is so open and with good stretches of visibility along here, and yet she had not noticed the motorbike coming up behind her – it just suddenly seemed to be there quite close to her car.

She was travelling at around 60mph, so it was feasible a bike travelling fast could catch up to her, but it seemed odd and bothered her a little that it just suddenly seemed to be right there on her tail as it were. She drove her car around a slight bend in the road, and as she did, the motorbike was just as suddenly no longer there behind her.

She actually became a bit concerned that perhaps the motorcyclist had lost control of his machine even though it wasn't a particularly dangerous bend, because she could not think of anywhere he might have safely turned off just there – especially if he was travelling at the presumably faster than 60mph he must have been doing in order to have caught her up in the first place.

She slowed and turned her car around in the forecourt of the Welton petrol station and went back to have a look, worrying that she would find a bike on its side on the road. There was nothing to be found, and she couldn't hear anything in the dark of the still night, even though she parked up and looked around for a few moments.

She turned the car back around and carried on home, but the whole incident bothered her so much she went back out first thing the next morning to have a proper look. It was still pricking at her that the rider might have come off and be lying hurt in the field, and she would be the only one who knew where they were. There was absolutely nothing to be found. No skid marks, no broken branches, no torn up grass, no debris. And most significantly, nowhere at all that the bike could have legitimately turned off.

She still often thinks about that night as she still regularly travels that stretch of road – but has never seen anything odd since.

ODIHAM CASTLE, Hampshire

The ruins of this lovely old castle, situated close to Odiham in Hampshire, are open to the public and are known locally as King John's Castle. The castle was in fact built by King John (he of the Magna Carta fame) on 20 acres of land which he had acquired from Robert the Parker, and which he modified by changing a bend in the River Whitewater. It took seven years to build, and was completed in 1214.

It remained in use as a castle for the first 100 years or so, but from then seems to have been mainly used as a prison – for one 11 year period from 1346 King David II of Scotland was held here after his capture at the Battle of Neville's Cross.

By the 1400s. It was being used mainly as a hunting lodge for the aristocracy, and by the 1500s it was already being described as a ruin. It was further destroyed in 1792 when the Basingstoke Canal was constructed through the southern corner of the plot.

Legend has it that the remains are haunted by the sound of someone playing a lute, and that you can sometimes hear the sound of marching.

One paranormal investigator told me of her experience there. She went down to the ruins one evening in 1997 with her husband, and stood in the middle of the site quietly observing her surroundings. It was a Thursday in September, so the evenings were drawing in but it was still quite pleasant as dusk fell: it had been a lovely sunny day with only a very light breeze, so they had not needed to wear jackets or coats.

Suddenly, from above her, there came the sound of a lute playing and people laughing, as if there were some sort of entertainment going on. Yet the place is just a ruin now, and there is no upper floor still standing. Her husband clearly heard the music and chatter too, and agreed that although there were no upper floors remaining, the sound definitely seemed to be coming from above them.

Although they have visited since, they have never heard the sounds again.

Several other people said that they had grown up in the area, and even though some had camped there as children, they had never seen or heard anything supernatural or inexplicable.

One lady told me that her grandmother took a photograph of the castle once on a visit, and it shows someone standing in one of the upper floor window frames - even though, as already established, there is no floor there anymore and therefore no-one could possibly have been standing there.

OLDHAM, Greater Manchester - BUTTERFLIES NIGHTCLUB

In 1908, the Grand Theatre in Oldham opened its doors to the public, and entertained its clientele with shows and plays for the next 30 years.

In 1936, work started on updating the building and converting it into a Cinema - since moving pictures were the new rage and making big money. The story goes that one worker had a dream that he was going to be crushed to death by a wooden beam falling at the site - and that he was so scared by his premonition that he stayed away for a couple of days. Of course, finances meant he couldn't stay away long, and so he reluctantly returned. Just a couple of days later the ropes gave way on a large beam which was being lowered into place - and just as he had predicted he was crushed and killed.

The belief is that his spirit continued to haunt the building ever afterwards, and that film of the ghost was actually caught on CCTV cameras in 1991.

By then, the building had been converted again, and it now housed Butterflies Nightclub and Rileys Snooker Club, having spent a while as The Astoria Ballroom (where apparently The Beatles once played in the 1960s).

The manager and deputy manager were in the habit of locking the building up together each night at closing time - and they would do so by making a systematic search of the building from top to bottom, making sure that no partygoers were still lingering anywhere to get inadvertently trapped inside. Once they were certain it was empty, they would lock all the doors and shut everything down, and set the alarm system and CCTV going.

On this particular night they had performed their usual routine, and had left the building when they got a call from the Police to say the alarm was sounding. Returning immediately, they turned off the alarms and again searched the building thoroughly from top to bottom, assuming with dismay that they must have missed someone in their first sweep of the building. After all, when you perform a routine function every time, it's easy to become accidentally a little complacent about it. However, to their puzzlement they found no-one inside and when they made further checks, they could find no sign of any attempted break in either.

They decided to watch the CCTV, since they had not been gone very long and therefore there wouldn't be much footage to watch, and to their astonishment saw the misty figure of a man walking through the corridors. They called in the local papers who ran an article on the event, and whose reporter took a couple of photos of paused stills of the CCTV images, in order to have a photo for the article. They sent the tape off for analysis, and although the company were able to confirm they found no evidence of tampering or double exposure, unfortunately the tape itself seems to have been lost. The only thing still remaining today is the still shots which the paper took.

When I asked locally, I was told that the building had gone through many iterations over the years: Bailey's Nightclub, Romeo and Juliet Nightclub, Top Rank, Froggies, Butterflies, and now there is a Roller Derby there.

Although many people wrote in with their memories of the place in its glory days from various decades, interestingly very few of them had ever experienced anything. One person remembered that his father's friend had worked as a bouncer there, and had seen some "creepy stuff" going on which eventually made him leave his job. One gentleman wrote in who had actually worked as a doorman there in the 1980s, with fond memories of how it was a "big" venue then, with well-known names like Showaddwaddy, Edwin Starr and so on headlining. He recalled that it had a reputation for being haunted, and said it was always really cold in the areas not open to the public, with a feeling that you were "being watched".

Then curiously, one chap wrote who said that the whole episode in 1991 had been a hoax, set up to try and create publicity for the venue, but when I tried to investigate, he declined to give any more detail.

One gentleman told me that he had worked there from 1980 until 1983. At that point in its life it was Romeo and Juliets nightclub. He described how behind the public areas, the whole building was a veritable rabbit warren of twisting corridors with doors leading off. He told me that these doors would often open and close by themselves, and although people tried to dismiss it as just air movement, it was clear that there was more to it than that by the way the doors behaved.

He said the building always had a really eerie feeling in the "back of house" areas, and lots of little things would happen all the time, like objects moving from where they were left and reappearing elsewhere. He remembered one particular evening when he had problems with his keys there. He worked at the bar, and it was his job to stock the bar and keep everything secure as well as serve. On one particular evening, he had arrived at the bar and been busy stocking up prior to opening time, but when he turned around to grab his keys, they were gone. Puzzled, since he had been working alone the entire time, he searched everywhere - and eventually found them in the staff room.

Not so unusual - except he had not left the bar area, had not been to the staff room, and no-one else had come in the entire time he had been there working...

PANTGWYNLAIS, Wales

Pantgwynlais today is a village suburb right on the very edge of Cardiff in south Wales, at the foot of the start of the area known as "The Valleys". Traditionally this whole area was rich in the history and tradition of coal mining, with the valleys themselves being a line of north/south valleys which were heavily populated by the miners and their families, who mined the mountains in between each valley line.

There used to stand here in Pantgwynlais a Gothic style mansion called Greenmeadows, which was the family seat of the Lewis family. They owned huge estates across south Wales, including a castle.

The property was eventually demolished in the 1940s after its ruins became dangerously hazardous, and on the site was built a pleasant housing estate of more modern homes and flats. The main house originally stood on the inside of the sharp bend which is on what is now called Greenmeadow Drive.

The area is thought to abound still in ghosts relating back to the days of the mansion, and several people came forward to tell me what they knew.

One lady explained that her aunt used to live in a flat built on part of the site during the 1970s. It was a pleasant enough property, with a view over the adjacent woodland, but it seemed her aunt shared the home with something inexplicable.

On one particular night, as the aunt lay in bed trying to get to sleep, she felt the room drop in temperature and the sensation of a cold "presence" coming into the room. There was no breeze or draughts, particularly as all the windows and doors were securely closed and locked up for the night. It was such a defined feeling of a definite entity that she actually sat up in her bed and asked "What do you want?" There was no answer, and the feeling of a presence dissipated.

My correspondent said that her aunt only had that experience once, but she heard from relatives of the people that moved in after her aunt left that they too had some strange experiences. They had woken up one morning and started going about their daily routine, but on walking into their lounge found that the net curtains at the window had been taken down and placed on a nearby chair, and all the videos which were normally lined up on a nearby shelf had been pulled off and scattered around the floor.

On another occasion, the family were awoken in the middle of the night when one of their child's toys, an automaton which played music, was suddenly turned on and started eerily playing away to itself even though everyone was fast asleep.

My witness had also heard local gossip about one of the houses opposite the flats having things move on their own accord around the mantelpiece in the lounge, and that the owners of the house had resorted to "getting someone in to deal with it".

I was directed by the locals to look up the other accounts about the hauntings in the area, and found an account explaining that in 1974 there was a newspaper report of a ghost haunting a council house which had been built on the land where the Greenmeadows Mansion had once stood. This account detailed that the ghost was known as The White Lady, and dated back to events in the 1840s, when a maidservant at the Mansion had fallen in love with a tinker who passed through the area on his regular route.

He was known as "Magpie" because of his habit of wearing a black jacket and white waistcoat, and the legend is that he persuaded the gullible young maid to become his accomplice in theft. She stole some of the family silver at his behest, and he sold the items and moved on - leaving her behind to face the consequences when the crime came to light. She tried to throw herself on the family's mercy, but they handed her over to the due process of the law, and she was found guilty and hanged for her crime.

The house was also said, according to the book, to have been haunted by a knight, a man wearing green (possibly the family's livery colours), and a hunchbacked man.

I also found a blog account of tales of the haunting of the original Mansion, which mentioned the same list of ghosts, as well as the tale of an old gardener who worked on the estate and knew that "something evil" lurked in one part of the gardens. He would warn the children of the house to stay away from that area, but eventually he must not have listened to his own warning, since both his body and those of his working dogs were found lying dead in that very area one day.

Another witness told me that he had encountered something paranormal on the estate, and yet another mentioned that the woods nearby were still haunted and had many myths associated with them.

PAKEFIELD, Suffolk – FLORENCE ROAD

I found a source story which described how this suburban seaside town side street was haunted by the sound of running footsteps at 9pm every evening. The street today is an eclectic mix of homes with different building styles and from different eras.

When I asked locally for any experiences of a haunting in that road, I got an interesting mix of answers. Some people had never heard of anything supernatural to do with the location even if they had lived there for several decades, whereas others were aware of the story of the footsteps.

Fascinatingly, a gentleman then contacted me to say that he was the person who had collected the original story from the witness back in 1973. He explained that the lady would hear footsteps running past her house every evening at the same time, but even when she stood outside watching there was never anyone to be seen.

One gentleman said that he had heard that it was an alleyway that runs between two of the houses on the street that was supposed to be haunted. Piecing together the information that the two correspondents gave me, it looks likely this is the rough side street called Long Acre according to the online maps readily available. The gentleman witness told me that he had heard it was said to be the ghost of a woman who screams, then runs down the alley towards the sea, looking in vain for her husband who was a sailor (and whom, one can suppose, had just been reported lost at sea?)

My witness said that a lot of local people had heard it, but although he himself was local he had never heard it himself. Another gentleman told me that his mother-in-law used to live in Florence Road and had heard the running steps.

Another witness said that the ghost was known as Crazy Mary, and that she follows the path from Florence Road to Pakefield Beach via the pathway by Pakefield Lighthouse in Pontins Holiday Centre (about a mile or so as the crow flies).

This directed me to a record of the legend, which says that the lighthouse at Pakefield was there to light the way for sailors passing through Pakefield Gateway, the channel between two shifting sandbanks which offered safe passage to Lowestoft harbour. The cliffs along here used to have a deep ravine between them (much eroded now) which was known as Crazy Mary's hole, and it was said to be the spot where the ghost of a widow driven crazy by grief waits, wringing her hands, for her drowned sailor husband to come home.

Apparently her ghost has been seen there for the last couple of decades, and soldiers during the Second World War would not man the defence watches there alone because of the fear of seeing the wailing ghost.

It seems quite possible that Crazy Mary starts her haunt by running towards these cliffs then and is only heard as footsteps at first, but later manifests more fully when reaching her destination?

PEWSEY, Wiltshire – THE FRENCH HORN PUB

I came across mention by local people corresponding with me of this former pub being haunted when researching for my previous books.

I followed up on the information by asking locally about any experiences, and came up with some interesting information. One lady told me that she had researched the property, and had found that it was originally built in the 1860s as a roadside house for the French prisoners of war who were being put to work digging out the final stretch of the nearby Kennett and Avon Canal. At the end of the day a horn would be sounded to signal that they could return to the lodging house, and thus the Inn was named after this practice.

Apparently, the ghost is that of a former landlady who was in the habit of popping her head around the door leading into the bar area as if still checking that everything was running smoothly. Occasionally, there is also the disembodied sound of a crying baby.

Today, the attractive red brick property is no longer a pub and its possible future seems uncertain, but quite a few people responded to my query with memories of time spent there.

One lady told me that she had spent the night at The French Horn a couple of times in years gone by, and had always felt that the place had a real "atmosphere". She said it was never as noticeable in the bar area when there were people around drinking and chatting, but upstairs in the private areas was a different matter.

She said you could sit up there sometimes and there would be a really pervasive feeling of unease in the air, and things would bump and bang as if someone else was moving around on the same floor, even though you knew you were up there alone.

Another lady remembered that it was haunted by The Grey Lady (possibly the same ghost of the former landlady?) and also by the ghosts of bargemen who used to frequent it as part of their lives on the busy canal.

A couple of people wrote to say they had worked there as bar staff for some years, one as far back as the 1980s, and they had never heard anything about it being haunted. This included one lady who said she lived there for a year and never experienced anything odd at all. One lady said she often used to go there for a meal, and had never picked up on anything strange about its atmosphere or any sense that anything otherworldly was there.

One person wrote to say that she used to know the girl whose family lived in the house directly next door to the pub - and this girl had told her that their home was haunted by smugglers from the canal - which makes it possible that there is some sort of link between the two properties and any ghosts.

And yet another witness wrote in to say they themselves had lived in the cottage next door for over 18 years, and once found a secret room behind a false wall. They thought it might have been used, once upon a time in the house's long history, as a hiding hole for smugglers. All that remained in it when they opened the room up was a very old cup and bowl.

She said that she used to do a lot of babysitting next door for the owners of the French Horn back in the late 1980's and early 1990's, and that she had a lot of very strange things happen whilst she was upstairs looking after the children. This would tend to correlate with the other witness who said the atmosphere was really only in the upstairs part of the building, not the public bar areas. She had also heard a tale that there was an underground tunnel which once connected the pub and the cottage.

PICKERING CASTLE, North Yorkshire

Dating back to the years of the Norman Conquest from 1069 onwards, Pickering Castle was originally a motte and bailey castle built from timber and earth. Over the years, like many of its counterparts, it was replaced by a stonework castle, added to and further fortified as the centuries went by. Its position, with a steep cliff on the west side, gave it a great advantage as a defensive structure. Assaults on the castle itself were made even more difficult by the deep defensive ditches that were dug around its outer walls.

Today, it is quite remarkably well preserved given its age, but this is largely due to the fact that it did not play a particularly active role in either the English Civil War or the War of the Roses, which meant it did not take as much heavy damage as many of its peers.

It has for many long years boasted the reputation of being haunted by a monk who is seen drifting through its ground with his arms outstretched, as if he is carrying something.

One witness told me that around 2009 she was out one day in the early afternoon walking her dog around the edges of the castle (which is a site open to the public), and heard the sound of a horse coming up close behind her. Pulling her dog in close to her heels with his leash, she stepped into the grass verge to make way for the rider, and then turned to look at them as they approached.

There was nothing there.

The same lady was out walking her dog around the front of the castle site on another occasion at about 10am one bright morning, when she suddenly noticed a large sphere of white mist hanging above the moat. It was a distinctly formed area of mist, and it was drifting slowly towards her – so that she was able to watch it for some time and marvel at its strangely perfect spherical shape. She was so surprised at the form of it that she actually took her glasses off and checked them for smears to make sure the shape was truly that of the mist itself and not an optical illusion. She said that it appeared to be about three feet in diameter. She has never seen anything like it before or since.

She lived at the time in one of the cottages not far from the castle. In order to reach the street from her front door, there was a narrow stone passage to walk down. On one occasion, she had clipped her dogs leash on to take him out to perform his toilet, and had entered the passageway, when suddenly a wall of thick white mist swept up the narrow corridor and enveloped her and the dog. She described it as so thick, and fast in its movement towards them, that she actually flinched and ducked as it came up the passage. At first she thought nothing much of it – but seconds later she reached the end of the passage and stepped out into a cool, clear, crisp, completely mist free night....

One person wrote in to say that there was a legend that a ghostly monk would walk around the moat at midnight, and as teenagers, local children would often dare each other to go and wait by the moat to see if they could see the spectre. Another remembered that the story was about a female spirit known by some as Mad Mary and by others as White Annie, who would apparently only appear at certain times of the year. There was a rumour that saying her name three times would conjure her spirit – but they said they had tried that to no avail.

POTBRIDGE, Hampshire

Potbridge is a tiny little hamlet in Hampshire, close to Odiham. There are probably only about a dozen houses there. One witness wrote to me to explain that in 1980, she and her family went to live in a beautiful 16th Century cottage in the village, and got rather more than they bargained for.

They moved in, and began to settle into their new home, unpacking their boxes over the next few days and deciding where they would arrange and store their belongings to make themselves comfortable and cosy.

At first, everything seemed perfectly normal, but a short while after they moved in, they were awoken suddenly in the middle of the night by the sound of voices. They sat up in bed, and could make out the sound of a man and a woman having a conversation together – but could not hear the voices clearly enough to actually determine what they were saying.

The sound came, as far as they could ascertain, from the kitchen area of the cottage, but although they naturally got up and investigated, they could find nothing to explain what they had heard.

At first they dismissed it, and assumed that a couple must have been walking home late or something and the sound of them chatting had simply carried on the breeze or whatever.

However, over the next few weeks, the experience was repeated on a number of occasions - and every time they could find nothing to account for the voices. After a few months, the sound of the voices gradually became less frequent, and eventually they heard them no more.

The cottage itself was semi-detached, and the adjoining property was originally the home of two elderly brothers who had lived there since the 1920s. One of the brothers had died not long before our witness and her family moved in next door, but the other remained next door for several more years before needing to move into a nursing home.

This meant that the property next door was eventually left empty, but it wasn't long after that happened before disturbances from it started. At around 8pm in the evening, there was a knocking on the party wall between the two houses, as if someone was trying to get their attention. It lasted for a few minutes, and was a quite definite sound. Although they checked around, there was no sign of anyone about and the empty property was still closed up tight and safe.

This went on for several evenings, and on the last occasion it was heard, the sound went on for much longer. This time, she described it has having a more frantic, even angry sense to the way the knocking sounded. The property was sold around that time, and she has often wondered whether it was the ghost of the deceased brother either angry at the fact that the house was being sold, or angry that he couldn't find his brother there anymore.

On one occasion, when our witness' mother was staying over, she awoke with a start in the middle of the night to see the figure of a man wearing what she described as a brown cloak standing by the inglenook fireplace. Quite a sensible woman, her mother was not frightened by the apparition but more intrigued about who it might be.

Despite their experiences, the witness describes it as "a lovely place to live" and has not been put off by their occasional supernatural shenanigans.

PURTON, Near Swindon, Wiltshire

A friend told my family this particularly creepy story.

She lived in Purton, in Wiltshire at the time, and was driving home in the wee small hours having been at a nightclub in Swindon for a pleasant evening out with friends.

One of her friends was going to stay the night with her, and was therefore in the passenger seat of the car with her. Our witness was the designated driver for their group, and so was stone cold sober, but her passenger had enjoyed a few too many perhaps and was snoozing peaceably in the warm interior of the heated modern car.

As she drove through the windy rural lanes close to home, she suddenly saw ahead of her two completely spherical balls of mist hanging motionless in the middle of the road. She was mildly puzzled to see them, since until that point the night had been perfectly clear with no hints of mist anywhere, and also, although mists forming are a fairly common phenomena of English weather, forming in the shape of a perfectly spherical ball is rather less usual.

Nevertheless, she drove through the two balls, which were hanging at about the same height as the interior cab of her car.

To her astonishment, as the vehicle passed through them, the temperature within the cab dropped sharply, so that for a moment it went completely icy cold, even though all the windows were shut and the vents were all closed.

The sudden drop was so noticeable that her drunken friend shivered in her sleep and awoke with a start, exclaiming loudly "What was that?"

Starting to tell her about the mist, the driver glanced into the rear view mirror to see absolutely nothing - the two strange balls of mist had completely disappeared.

QUINTRELL DOWNS, Cornwall

Quintrell Downs is a village in Cornwall not far from the popular beach resort of Newquay, but a little inland. It has quite a mixture of modern and older buildings, and is not a particularly large village. One witness wrote in to tell me about her father in law, who seemed to cause enough of a stir there after his death to leave the whole family feeling sure that life after death is a very real thing.

Naturally, the family were devastated at the loss of their beloved family member, but very soon after his death they noticed that some very strange things started to happen.

Firstly, the watch he had worn for many years and which he was wearing on the day he died, stopped working the moment he died and refused all attempts to get it going again. Giving up, his wife put it away carefully in a drawer of their bedside cabinet. A few days later, she went into the bedroom whilst busying herself with her day to day chores, and discovered the watch lying in the middle of the bedroom floor!

On the day he died, his grieving widow also took off her wedding ring and put it away for safekeeping. When she went to retrieve it, to her absolute heartbreak, she found that it had inexplicably gone missing. The whole family helped her to search for it over the next few days, because she was understandably desperate to be able to wear it to his funeral. Their search was to no avail, for despite all their efforts they could not find it anywhere.

Then on the day of the funeral, his widow went to retrieve another item of jewellery kept in the same place as the ring had been so carefully placed and then went missing from – only to find the ring innocently sitting there in plain sight!

A few days later, our witness' three year old daughter, the deceased's granddaughter, woke up in the middle of the night and complained about the man that was standing by the door in her bedroom.

The incident with the ring reminds me of an experience myself and my husband had. He keeps his own wedding ring on a shelf in our lounge, because he works outdoors with plant and machinery and rings are a dangerous thing to wear in that sort of situation. He tends to simply put it on when we are going out for the evening.

About three years ago, he looked for the ring one evening, and could not find it anywhere. Over the next couple of months, I took the lounge apart piece by piece looking for it, even moving the furniture and emptying all the shelves and drawers. Eventually I had to admit defeat and concluded it must somehow have been picked up with a piece of rubbish and thrown away, or sucked up by the hoover. I gave my poor husband quite a telling off for being careless with it and not putting it away properly in its box each time.

For his birthday the following year, I bought him a new one. I managed to find one which I thought was very similar to his original, which was an intricate Celtic knot design, albeit a bit slimmer in width and a bit more delicate.

A few weeks later, my cleaner (a young lass in her teens who I was helping out with her first "job" as her mother is one of my friends) was helping me clean the lounge. She picked his wedding ring up off the shelf and asked where she should put it as I had asked her to dust and tidy the shelving unit.

Feeling quite cross – I called out to my husband and told him he should have put it away in its box, or the same thing would happen as last time. Puzzled, he came into the lounge, and said, "but it *is* in the box!" Glaring at him in the way only wives can do, I held the offending ring out to show him. Glaring back – he lifted the wedding ring box down from its place on the shelf and opened it – to reveal his "new" wedding ring sitting safely inside.

I was holding his old ring. Which was sitting there, in plain sight, right on the shelf where it had been lost three years earlier. The shelf which had been taken apart piece by piece searching for it. Which had been cleaned dozens of times, and ornaments changed and moved dozens of times over the intervening months. We just stared at the two rings in complete astonishment.

And, incidentally, the new ring I had found was an *exact* match for the original!

RAUNDS, Northamptonshire

One gentleman told me that in 1981 his beloved father, who worked as the driver of a recovery tow truck, was killed whilst attending a call out at the side of the road. He was tragically struck by a passing vehicle.

Although this was a devastating blow for his family, of course life must go on and so in due course my witness met the lady who was to become his wife, and they started living together in a modern three bedroom house they found in the small town.

One day his wife woke up at around 3am in the morning needing to visit the bathroom – and saw a man standing in their bedroom for a brief moment before he disappeared. Terrified, she woke her new husband up, and when she described what she had just seen, he was able to recognise the description of his deceased father – who had died before he and his wife had ever met.

On another occasion, again at around 3am in the morning, my witness got out of bed to go and let their cat out who was meowing impatiently. As he walked into their lounge, for a brief moment he saw his father sitting comfortably on their sofa, relaxing with his legs crossed at the ankle just as he used to in life. Just before the figure disappeared, he realised that he could not discern the shape of his father's head or arms, even though he was certain it was his father he was seeing just by the familiarity of the posture.

RETFORD, Nottinghamshire –

AMBULANCE STATION NORTH ROAD

There is an ambulance station on North Road in Retford. It is a modern building, long and low, with several bay doors for the ambulances, and a resident ghost.

One paramedic working there wrote to me to say they think it might be a former member of staff, because they hear his cheerful whistling coming from empty rooms. On other occasions, someone will think that a person has just walked in to the kitchen area, and offer them a cup of tea, then look up to find no-one is actually there. Sometimes, the ambulance bay doors open on their own, and on other occasions, items in the stores are mysteriously rearranged. She herself has actually witnessed the bay doors open even though no-one was there.

Several other people remembered that the ghost had been known there for quite a few decades, and that it was particularly bay door 3 which used to go up by itself, and footsteps were often heard in the empty garage.

Another lady told me that she used to work there in the 1980s and although she herself never experienced anything she couldn't explain, she remembered that other staff who worked there at the same time reported experiencing odd things. She said that it was never frightening to anyone.

One witness remembered being in the ladies loo there once, at least ten years ago or more, when someone rapped sharply on the cubicle door - even though she knew the room beyond was in fact empty. It took her a little while to pluck up the courage to actually leave the cubicle!

Some other witnesses then came forward to mention the ghost of a lady in white who was seen on the stairs at Retford Hospital by one of the cleaners who worked there. There was a general agreement that the place can feel quite eerie at night. A former security guard commented that it was definitely haunted when he worked there, and another lady said that when she worked there, eerie noises would sometimes be heard that they could find no explanation for. On other occasions, people reported seeing shadows move in the corridors.

RISELEY, Bedfordshire

I wrote about the roads around Risely and the hauntings along them in my previous book, "The Roadmap of British Ghosts". Whilst researching for that book, I was given a couple of extra interesting snippets which I didn't include since that book specifically covered the ghosts which haunt our highways and byways.

One gentleman told me that he was in the pub in the village, The Fox and Hounds, one evening, and visited the men's toilets. Whilst he was in one of the stalls, he heard someone else open the "main" door to the toilets and enter. He could hear their footsteps and them moving around, even as he finished up his own business and exited the stall he was in.

He expected to see another customer as he left his cubicle and went to wash his hands. To his astonishment, since the noises had been right that second, there was no one else in the toilet area.

He told me that normally he doesn't believe in "this sort of thing" but admits he still feels quite baffled by his experience because the sound was so clear, and so mundane, except for the fact that it turned out no one was there.

This sparked another person to say they had lived in the pub for a number of years, and had all sorts of strange things happen in the time they were there. Another lady said she worked there as a barmaid for several years and would hear similar stories from customers from time to time, and actually herself experienced something very similar whilst alone in the cellar one shift: the sound of someone else coming into the area, and then finding out she was in fact alone.

I went ghost hunting a few times around the lanes of Risely, sometimes on my own and sometimes taking a friend with me. On one of those evenings, we stopped at the pub to use its loos, and bought an orange juice each just to be polite since we were using its facilities. My friend, who had not seen the extra snippets from my research, since we were out looking for the main haunting detailed in the previous book, came out of the ladies loo and said she would rather if we went and sipped our drinks on the patio outside while she had a smoke - because the loos had just freaked her out a bit because while she was there she thought she had heard someone else come in, and yet there was no-one there..

On another of my jaunts to the area, this time in the middle of the afternoon with my two dogs, I was walking round the edge of one of the fields close to the main site of the haunting I was researching at the time. I was visiting it specifically in daylight and with dogs, because it had been experienced by others under those conditions, and armed with a camera and EMF meter I was hoping to replicate their experience.

As I walked along, a farmer drove into the field in a pick-up truck and went about some business over against the farthest hedge. After a while, he got back into his vehicle and drove around the headland of the field to intercept me. (The headland is the large swathe of natural grass left around the edges of fields to provide an area for wildlife to nest and thrive whilst the rest of the field is cropped.) Wondering why he wanted to talk to me, since I was on a public footpath and my dogs were on leads, I stood and politely waited for him.

He joined me, and it turned out he just wanted to warn me that there had been a lot of thefts from parked cars in the area and to be careful not to leave my car unattended for too long.

We ended up chatting for quite a while, and I explained to him what I was doing and asked if he had ever seen or heard the haunting I was out looking for.

He had not, but told me an interesting story. He explained that a couple of fields away from where we were standing, there used to be a farmhouse which had a couple of cow sheds and other out-buildings around it. For many long decades it had been the home of a traditional old "small holding" farmer and his wife - they raised their children there, with a few milking cows and some hens, and a smallish plot of land - eking out an impoverished but typically rural lifestyle. In time, their children grew up and left home, and the old farmer and his wife stayed on in the property as it gradually became more and more dilapidated around them. The children, sadly, had shown no interest in carrying on in the same way of life and taking over the farm.

As the couple grew older, first their cows had to go as they could not care for the big beasts anymore, and then gradually they let the fields go as they became too old to tend to them too. Eventually the old man died, leaving his wife to live out her last few years in the ramshackle old farmyard with just her chickens and cats for company.

My informant, who had lived in the area and worked these fields all his life and was now himself an elderly, mostly retired man, was himself a young man when the old lady finally died, and the buildings fell further into disrepair and the farmhouse was eventually demolished.

For some years after, the cowsheds still stood, and he and his friends used to go there at dusk sometimes to do a bit of rat or rabbit shooting. He said that on a couple of occasions he either saw or heard the old lady calling her cats in and "chucking" to her chickens as she fed them, just the way she used to in life. On one evening, he rounded the corner and saw for a moment the apparition of the old farmer, still peaceably leaning against the gate to his farmyard and puffing away on his pipe.

ROWDE, Wiltshire

A lady wrote in to tell me about a very lovely experience with a possible ghost she once had whilst living in the small village of Rowde, not far from Devizes in Wiltshire.

She lived in a small row of old cottages, and would set out every day to take her German shepherd dog, San, out for its daily exercise. Most days, as she passed the last house in the row, the two old ladies who lived there would often stop her for a little chat and to pass the time of day. Invariably, they would kiss her cheek before she carried on her way.

Time passed, and eventually she learned with great sadness that one of the old ladies had passed away, leaving the other all alone.

The next time she stopped by to chat to the surviving lady, and offer condolences, as she went to leave, the old lady again offered a kiss to her cheek. As she did so, my witness distinctly felt another kiss being pressed to her opposite cheek - just as if both ladies had kissed her at once. She didn't say anything, for fear of causing upset, but says to this day she feels privileged to have felt that.

On another occasion, in 2005, she was out in the wee small hours of the night after finishing a shift, giving San the dog a last walk before she went to bed. It was only about four days before Christmas, and so it was cold and completely quiet at that time in the morning. She didn't bother putting her dog on a lead since no-one was about, and walked up Marsh Lane. She carried doggie bags with her and was watching carefully where her dog went to make sure she cleaned up any mess.

As they came level with the junction to Springfield Road, she noticed a tall man wearing a long dark coloured coat walking towards her up Marsh Lane. He didn't acknowledge her or speak, but she thought it was a little odd to see someone else out and about at that very late hour.

She turned into Springfield Road, and suddenly became aware of such an overpowering smell of cigarette smoke that it actually made her splutter and cough - just as you might if someone actually blew the smoke in your face. The smell was in a very localised spot underneath a street lamp, and by experimenting a little she found that she could literally step in and out of the affected area, which was only a couple of feet across.

The next night, working the same pattern, she was out again at the same time with her dog and walked the same route. Sure enough, there was the tall man in his dark coat again, and again he did not acknowledge her presence but carried on walking. Once again, in the same spot, she was assaulted by the strong, weirdly localised smell of cigarette smoke.

When she encountered him again on the third morning in a row, she decided to speak to him. She said "Morning! Isn't it cold?", and immediately felt slightly silly at her comment, because of course it was cold - it was the middle of the night in December. Nevertheless he politely answered her, saying, "Yes it is". As he went to walk on past, her dog San went to sniff at him, and she said, "Don't worry, he's friendly, he won't hurt you." The man ignored both her and the dog, and carried on walking. She turned to watch him walk away, saying, "Goodnight, Merry Christmas" as he went. He didn't reply but carried on walking - and vanished completely from sight just a few feet away from her. He didn't fade away - he just vanished all at once, as if someone had turned off an image.

She said that although it made the hair on the back of her neck stand up, she wasn't entirely surprised, as she'd had a feeling there was something not quite normal about the encounter or the way she kept seeing him at the same time and sensing the weirdly localised smoke.

Although she was often out at that time of night again, she never saw him after that.

RUGELEY, Staffordshire - ABBEYSOUND STUDIOS, HERON COURT HALL

I was contacted by a gentleman who owns and runs Abbeysound Studios in Rugeley. His business occupies the top floor of Heron Court Hall - what is left of a stunning looking old building dating from 1851.

Originally built by Joseph Whitgreave, a co-founder of nearby St Joseph and St Etheldreda Church (named after Joseph and his sister Etheldreda), Heron Court Hall was then occupied by the Sisters of the Christian

Retreat for around fifty years from 1903. It is a tall gabled house made of brick with stone dressings in the mid 1800s Tudor style - or "gothic". When built, it was considered one of the "greatest ornaments of the town".

The Sisters of the Christian Retreat originally opened St. Anthony's Convent at Heron's Nest, Heron Street, (just over the road) in 1901, but to accommodate additional nuns who had been expelled from France the convent was moved on 31 July 1904 to Heron Court Hall. They used it as a Christian retreat and a teaching centre.

In the mid 1870's, one entire wing of the building was demolished, leaving the central part which is all that remains today. In its place was built the Heron Court Congregational Church and school room. Both of these buildings were demolished in the 1970s due to subsidence - with the surrounding land being sold off for residential development

The building was then bought by the town's Billiards Club sometime in the 1960's, and our witness' business took on the tenancy of the top floor which he had converted into fully soundproof studio areas around 35 years ago in 1984.

When our witness moved his business into the property, he was told that the area he was to occupy was actually the former dormitory area for the young novice nuns. He was warned it was haunted, and told that it was the spirit of a nun who had committed suicide by hanging herself. He was also told that there used to be a tunnel running between Herons Court Hall and Heron's Nest.

Over the years that he has occupied the building, there have been sporadic occurrences which he cannot find any rational explanation for. Some of these he has experienced himself, and some have occurred to visitors to his business.

On a couple of occasions over the years, whilst working alone in the studio recording audio books, our witness has experienced the sensation of someone gently running their fingers through his hair. He has always had quite short hair, so the fingers trail over his actual scalp - and although to me that sounds horrifically creepy, he described it as actually not having any bad feeling to it at all. He says that he has never sensed or felt any malevolence – to him the interactions when they come always feel more like something is being playful or mischievous. A couple of people he has discussed it with over the years have asked him whether it was caused by static from all of the electrical equipment there is operating in the studio, but he is sure after all these years working in the same space that he can tell the difference.

On another occasion, he watched as a mirror unhooked itself from the wall. It was quite a large mirror, two or three feet across, and was attached to the wall by a hook which hung over a nail. In order to remove the mirror, either the nail would need to fall out of the wall, or bend downwards, or you would have to lift the hook up and over the nail.

On this day, he watched as the mirror did just that – lifted itself upwards and clear of the nail before falling to the floor.

On another occasion, he had a member of staff working or him who was a young girl on work experience. On this particular day, he wasn't expecting to see her as he would be out of the building when she was due to be in, but he left her a set of instructions for her duties on a piece of paper, which he clipped securely to a clipboard with a bulldog clip and left propped up where she would immediately find it.

When he next came in, the clipboard was over on one side of the studio, and the note with instructions was over on the other. Not thinking much of it, and assuming she had simply removed the note in order to work from it, he carried on getting the studio ready for the next piece of work and tidying round. In doing so, he flicked the answer machine messages on to see who had called and make a start on the day's business.

The first message was from his work experience girl, apologising that she would not be able to come into work as she was not feeling well.

This left him puzzled. If he had left the note securely affixed to the clipboard, propped up on one side of the studio – and his one and only member of staff had not in fact been into the building because she was sick ... then who had detached the note and moved both it and the clipboard to opposite sides of the studio?

He has also had customers who are using the studio tell him that they have put their guitars down on the floor for a moment, only to see them slide along the floor unaided. He said that one of his favourite occurrences happened when the lead singer of a rock band who were using the studio said to him, "Come on, haunting is a load of old nonsense. It's great for a bit of publicity to say your building is haunted, mate, but come on, really?"

At that precise moment, as the lead singer spoke, a clock affixed to the wall suddenly flung itself off the wall and hit him. From that moment on, this big, intimidating rock singer refused to go anywhere in the building unaccompanied – even to the toilets!

Over the years there have been numerous little incidents, but as our witness pointed out, in reality the occurrences are quite few and far between so there is no sense of spooky atmosphere to the building or anything like that.

It's not just the top floor which is affected either. One of his customers went down to the first floor where the snooker club runs a bar area, and was talking to the barmaid there whilst ordering a drink. He was saying to the barmaid, that actually he didn't think there was much to the tales of haunting that went with the building. She was agreeing with him, telling him that she had worked there for some time and had never experienced anything unusual. She then reached for the glass she had just poured for him to pass it over, but as she reached towards it, the glass just literally exploded.

Change in temperature perhaps? Warm glass affected by cold liquid? Maybe, maybe not.

Interestingly, considering the studio is by definition such a quiet still place, my witness says there is never a sense of cold spots or unease. Nor has any extraneous sound ever made its way onto any of his recordings, so EVP (Electronic Voice Phenomena) does not seem to be a feature of this case.

The activity seems to have died down a bit over the last couple of years - although it might just be that he has become accustomed to the funny little things that happen and pays less attention now.

Our witness told me that he has a friend who is interested in the paranormal and who has tried to look around the building, and in particular tried to find the tunnel which is supposed to exist between Heron Court Hall and nearby Heron's Nest. This friend has told our witness that when checking the building out they saw what appeared to be black shadow walk past the end of the corridor, and also caught the sound of something banging the drums when no-one was present! They did find what looked like a bricked up doorway down in the basement which might possibly be the entrance to the tunnels if they do in fact exist.

RUNCTON, Sussex.

One witness wrote in to tell me about his experiences when he was working in one of the many plant nurseries which are dotted around the small village of Runcton in West Sussex, sometime in the early 1990s.

He explained, "One night I was working late. It was my job to check the flow of water through all of the various irrigation systems." He knew that there were only three of the staff working that night - himself, a person working in the offices, and another over the other side in the other offices. The three of them kept in touch by walkie talkie, since the whole site covered some 11 acres.

He was working away, concentrating on the systems he was checking, but noticed one of the others walk by on the other side of the huge greenhouse. Just a moment later, one of his colleagues made him jump by coming up right beside him and saying that he had just come down to say goodnight before heading on out.

He gave a little embarrassed laugh that his colleague had made him jump, saying, "you got over here quick! I saw you go past on the other side just a moment ago!"

Puzzled, his colleague responded that he had not been over to the other side of the greenhouse all night, and he didn't think anyone else had either. As they looked at each other in slight puzzlement for a moment, it suddenly dawned on my witness that his colleague was dressed mostly in blue. The person he had seen had been wearing brown. He tried to laugh it off, saying he thought he might just have seen the ghost then.

He knew other workers had sometimes seen this lone figure walking around the huge greenhouses when no one living was there.

RUSHTON, Northamptonshire

When I was researching for "The Roadmap of British Ghosts", I was asking locally about the ghostly monk who is rumoured to haunt the A43 at Barford Bridge in Northamptonshire, a little way east of Rushton.

One lady contacted to tell me that she once lived at Storefield Cottages for six years, which are just off the roundabout junction of the A43 and the A6003. This is a small row of about a dozen terraced cottages, sat on their own and now slightly isolated by the convergence of the two roads.

She remembers when the road crews were there, digging out the footings for the new dual carriageway of the A43. She says that the workmen found a Roman burial ground there. Once the digging stopped, they seemed to trigger a number of ghostly happenings in the gardens of the houses, and sometimes even inside the back rooms which faced out that way.

She explained that they never really saw anything, but they would hear the sound of footsteps, and that these could clearly be heard pacing about as if on stone or tile, when in fact their flooring was made of cork, and deliberately designed to deaden sound, including that of footfalls, as well as provide insulation. She remembered that once the road was built there were many accidents, where people claimed to have seen the ghost of the monk standing near the bridge.

A gentleman wrote in to corroborate the story, saying that at the time the highway improvements were being made, the works were taking place in what used to be the fields at Keepers Lodge, where his family worked and owned the farm. He remembered the road crew and the archaeologists digging the holes to exhume the Roman skeletons in the 1970s prior to the roadwork being started, and that as children he and his siblings would play in and out of the holes that were left behind before the land was compulsorily purchased and the new road built.

SALFORD, Greater Manchester – THE OLD SALFORD ROYAL HOSPITAL

One gentleman wrote to me to say that many years ago, before it was closed down, he used to work at this old hospital.

Late one night he was working in an operating theatre, and while he worked, he could hear the sound of something creaking and smell cigarette smoke.

He said that the story he was told was that many years previously, a surgeon had made a terrible mistake one day and amputated the wrong leg from an injured patient. So filled with remorse was he by his mistake, that the surgeon smoked a last cigarette and the hung himself using a rope.

The creaking he had heard is thought to be the sound of the rope creaking as it swung with the weight of the body hanging from it.

SALISBURY, Wiltshire – DEBENHAMS, BLUE BOAR ROW

I found an account which said that Debenhams Department Store in Salisbury is haunted, and was intrigued enough to follow it up by asking locally.

Apparently, the store stands on what was formerly the site of the Blue Boar Inn, which itself was later renamed The Saracens Head. Supposedly, the site is haunted by Henry Stafford, 2nd Duke of Buckingham, who was beheaded in the square outside the building for treason against King Richard III in 1483. He allegedly spent his last hours locked in an attic room of the old building, and although that building is no longer there, his spirit continues to haunt the locale. There is a tale that a BT Phones engineer working on site suddenly felt a hand on his shoulder even though he was working alone. Apparently he was so terrified by his experience that he fled the building and vowed to never return, leaving someone else to go and clear up his tools for him.

There is also supposed to be the ghost of a little girl wearing Victorian style dress in the street immediately outside of the door.

One gentleman responded to my query, explaining that for a time he worked as a security guard there, and none of the guards would go up into what was known as The Duke's room on their own.

Another chap mentioned that he did some relief security work there for a couple of nights in the 1970's was not troubled by anything supernatural happening.

Then one witness wrote in to explain that he used to be the Security Manager there from 1999 to 2002. He remembered that the paranormal activity they sometimes experienced there would become more noticeable around October and November each year. He was there when the BT engineer mentioned in the source story I had found was working there. He said the man actually came out of the area he had been working in screaming, and was clearly in a state of shock. My witness was the First

Aider on site, and so he was called to help the man, who he said was shivering with cold and fright and was very pale and distressed. The BT Engineer was adamant that someone had touched him whilst he was working, and refused to go back in to the area he had been working on under any circumstances.

My witness explained that during that period he also had real trouble with the door alarms all over the building. In order to set the building alarms, all of the doors had to be closed and locked, and any of them being opened would trigger the alarm. On one such call out, he arrived back at the building in the middle of the night and checked the alarm instrumentation panel. It was indicating that there were intruders on the restaurant's kitchen staircase. Rushing to the area to check, they found that the door was open – although it must have been locked securely earlier in the evening, or the alarm would have refused to arm itself in the first place. There were no intruders.

On another occasion, he was working late one evening on the top floor. He knew there were five staff on duty in the building, and as he walked down the stairs at break time, he saw someone standing by the door to what is known as the Dukes Room. He didn't think too much of it as he carried on down to the canteen area – until he walked in and saw the other five staff members were already in there taking their break and realised he was the last down. So who had been standing outside the Duke's Room?

On another occasion, he arrived at work and made his customary inspection of the building, only to find that all of the chairs in the restaurant (one of the oldest parts of the building) were tumbled upside down in one corner of the room.

SHEFFIELD, Yorkshire

One witness wrote to tell me that he has lived in two different haunted houses in Sheffield.

The first was a property in Greenside Mews in Hackenthorpe. The previous owner had been an old gentleman who had recently passed away. He had been very proud of his beloved garden, which he kept in beautiful condition with flowering plants and attractive borders filled with scented roses.

Having moved in, our witness worked hard to restore the garden to its glory and to tend and nurture the roses the old man had been so proud of. She firmly believes that his spirit would come around to check on progress and keep an eye on his plants, because she would get sudden strong whiffs of cigar smoke accompanied by an inexplicable cold spot.

In time, the family moved on, and went to live in a house in Walkley in Sheffield. There, they often catch glimpses of two ghosts which appear to be two ladies wearing black or dark coloured clothing. Sometimes, they also walk into a room to catch sight of the witness' mother's elderly dog lying in his favourite spot in front of the kitchen cupboards - even though the dog passed away some years ago. She says she finds it quite comforting to think his spirit is lingering around the family, keeping them company and guarding them just as he did in life.

She has also caught a glimpse of a lady wearing red looking round the shower curtain at her when she has been taking a shower - rather more brave than I might have been in the same circumstances, she reacted by politely asking the spirit to give her some privacy in the bathroom!

Intrigued by their "companions" in this new house, they have been trying to research its history as it is quite an old building. They think they might have established that one of the ladies dressed in black might be the spirit of a dressmaker who lived there some time ago.

SHUGBOROUGH HALL, Staffordshire

Shugborough Hall is owned by the National Trust today and is open to the public as an attraction. The building which can be seen now is an elegant house built in around 1695, but it replaces a much earlier Bishop's Palace. This earlier medieval building was moated, but suffered the fate of many of England's religious properties during the Dissolution of the Monasteries under King Henry VIII, and passed into private ownership.

The estate was bought by William Anson in 1624 for a very costly sum for the times, and he was the one who first remodelled it. His grandson then remodelled again in 1693, resulting in the core of the building which you can visit now. It has been added to and restyled several times more over the intervening centuries, and some of the money to do this came from one of the family, Admiral George Anson, who circumnavigated the globe in his ship The Centurion during 1740 - 1744. He captured a Spanish treasure ship, and much of that wealth was ploughed into the Hall as the family's seat.

Some sources claim that the name Shugborough Hall derives from Shug: meaning a devil or evil spirit, and barrow: referring to an ancient type of burial mound. Its name can therefore allegedly be roughly interpreted to mean "Haunted Hill"

It is said to have its fair share of ghosts, of course; from a former housekeeper whose skirt still rustles in the kitchens, to Lady Harriet's spectre in the State Bedroom, where apparently she died whilst giving birth to her child.

One witness wrote to me to explain that they had once lived and worked at the Hall with their own mother and father. Naturally they had heard the stories of the Grey Lady ghost, and she was really hoping she might encounter the spirit as she firmly believes in the afterlife.

She would therefore deliberately walk around the house and enter rooms that had no visitors in them, hoping to catch a glimpse of the ghost. She had no luck with this tactic, but then one day they had a workman in the Hall completing some necessary maintenance.

Her mother was seated in the office as she too was working that day, when suddenly the workman came rushing in. He was in a distressed state, and told her mother rather agitatedly that "something or someone was trying to get him out of the house and was trying to hurt him" - and promptly left - refusing to ever come back.

Not long after that incident, our witness saw the ghost herself. She was walking up the stairs into the flat where they lived, having just come home very late from a night out, and she stopped by the alcove where they kept their coats and shoes, in order to take her shoes off. As she bent down to remove her shoes, she glimpsed to her left the bottom half of the Grey Lady's dress, who seemed to be standing quite close to her. As soon as she stood back up in surprise, the shape had disappeared.

The next time our witness saw the ghost was late one night, after she had already gone to bed. She woke at around 2am, to see the Grey Lady walk through the wall which separates the bedroom from their bathroom, across the foot of her bed between the bed and the window, and through the other wall, which led onto offices.

The offices themselves have motion sensor alarms in them, but the ghost did not trigger the alarms.

Our witness said she did not feel frightened as she saw the ghost - she just lay in bed afterwards wondering if that had really just happened.

And finally, one one occasion she was playing around with her phone and trying out a new app which records sound - and when she played it back it had caught a man's voice saying "hello!", even though no-one else was present at the time.

SISSINGHURST, Kent

One lady wrote to me to tell me about her family's experience whilst living in a house in Sissinghurst, not far from Tunbridge Wells in Kent.

She and her two children and then family cat lived in the house for around ten years, and although most of the time it was a reasonably pleasant place to live, it also had its darker side.

They shared the home with four ghosts – two young children, an old man, and occasionally an old lady.

They would catch glimpses of the two children sitting on the stairs, seemingly watching the family going about their daily routine. They seemed to be there quite frequently, although there was nothing, as she put it, "horrible or untoward" about their presence.

While her son was very small, it seemed that the ghostly children would go into his bedroom at night and play with his toys – moving them about and turning them on. As he grew older, by the age of about six, he started to be able to see them, and they would try and play with him.

The ghost of the old man was a different matter altogether. When seen, his expression would seem to be more of someone leering, as opposed to just looking. She would feel his presence follow her up the stairs sometimes, and to her it felt more like being chased up the stairs. She tried to tell herself it was nonsense, but that was not how it felt.

She said that although life went on as normal, it was only once they moved out that they really realised what a strain living with the ghosts had been putting them under – with the constant feeling of being on slight tenterhooks that something might be about to happen.

She was made aware in later years that the house had once suffered from a tragic fire, and that two children had died there from smoke inhalation. The old man ghost was that of a former resident, who didn't die at the property but seemed to be reliving his time there, and the old lady ghost, who mostly frequented the kitchen, had also been someone who lived there in previous years.

Occasionally, she would see other spirits in the house, but usually only once for each – which makes me wonder if the house was some sort of easy conduit for the paranormal.

SLEIGHTS, Yorkshire

Sleights is a small village, just a couple of miles inland from the famous old coastal town of Whitby, with its links to Count Dracula. Sleights is a fascinating name for a village, which finds its roots in Old Norse, "sletta" meaning "flat lands".

A lady wrote in to tell me about an experience they had whilst on holiday there one year about 25 years ago – probably in the early 1990's. The family, consisting of herself, her husband, their four children, her mother and aunt, and the family's two dogs would normally all holiday together in Scotland. However, one particular year, she was rather late in getting around to booking their accommodation, and found that they could not have their usual destination. With such a large party, of course, holiday rental choices are a bit more limited, so she asked the company they liked to use what they had left for the week they had in mind.

The holiday company suggested a Grade II listed Victorian house in Sleights in Yorkshire, which was both big enough and available at the time they wanted. They had a look at the details, and thought it looked as if it would meet their needs very nicely, so they signed up and booked the holiday.

When they arrived, they found the accommodation to be very clean and comfortable, but a little bit limited, so she and her husband were to share a family room with their two youngest children. This wasn't a problem, as they were glad to be able to be all taking a holiday together, and it was quite a large spacious room in the old house, with a good sized double bed and two singles.

The holiday progressed without incident at first, but in the middle of the week things started to turn a little strange. The family had all retired for the night, but the two youngest seemed unusually restless. Mum and Dad lay with the lights out in their room, trying to encourage the little ones to sleep, but their five year old daughter in particular seemed very reluctant to drop off to sleep, so they allowed her to climb into bed with them to help her try and settle.

After a while, the little girl did fall asleep, but this left our witness feeling a bit cramped and hot with the three of them in bed, and as she was now struggling to fall asleep herself, she decided that rather than disturb the sleeping child, she would get out of the double bed and go and sleep in the now vacated single bed in the room.

She lay awake for some time, not feeling particularly sleepy, when something disturbed her. Looking across the room, she saw a young girl in a white nightdress walking towards her. Assuming it was her daughter wanting to get back in her own bed, she scooted back a bit, lifted the duvet in invite, and said "Come on in then."

At this point, as our witness was looking directly at her, she saw the young girl just fade away.

Startled, she leapt out of bed and opened the door to let the light from the landing spill into the room. Her daughter and husband were both still fast asleep in the double bed.

Although she told the adults in the group what she had seen, there was nothing more to be said or done about it, but interestingly, when they came to write in the visitors book they saw that one page had been torn out, and the page immediately after it had the entry "Didn't see a ghost, but had a lovely stay". She has often wondered whether the missing page had referenced the ghost, hence the next person to stay "responded" by mentioning that they had *not* seen it: but the owners tore the page out so as not to frighten future guests...

Interestingly, when discussing with her husband that she was thinking of writing to me after seeing my plea for people's own experiences, she asked him whether he believed her when she said she had seen the ghost of the small child.

He finally admitted that he did - because he had seen her too!

SOUTHEND ON SEA, Essex – SEAVIEW ROAD

Composed mostly of terraced cottages, this small suburban side street in Southend on Sea, not far from the actual seafront, housed some paranormal activity in one of the newer properties.

My witness told me that in the early 1990s, she and her family lived down this street. There was one room upstairs which seemed to always attract the activity, and as the family swapped bedrooms over the years, they each experienced something in that same room.

Her husband saw "something" he couldn't really define hovering in the middle of the room one night, before it promptly disappeared.

A few years later that bedroom belonged to their teenage daughter, who was woken in the middle of the night by a slight noise. Looking over, she saw a young boy sitting on the floor and looking through her record collection. At first she thought it was her younger brother – but realised shortly afterwards that it wasn't.

A few years later still, and her son was now using the room which his older sister had vacated, and complained that he too "saw something hovering" in the middle of the room in the middle of the night.

ST NEOTS, Cambridgeshire

One gentleman wrote to me with his experience from a few years ago, when he himself was around 20 years of age.

He recalled that it was in the month of June, and that he had met a girl through the popular social media site "Facebook". She was Irish, and the two of them became quite good friends. She happened to be living in St Neots as a children's nanny for the son of a man who was employed as a train driver and who therefore worked long and unsociable hours sometimes.

She invited her friend, our witness, to go and keep her company one evening and hang out with her as she babysat. The two friends sat together on the sofa in the living room, and the young Nanny was telling how her services were needed because her employer's wife had passed away, leaving him to care for their young son alone. The wife had been cremated after her death, and her ashes were kept in a decorative funerary pot upstairs. His friend told him that she thought the late wife might still be haunting the house because she sometimes heard footsteps emanating from upstairs.

My witness said that although he listened politely to his friend and her tale, inside he was busy thinking "Whatever. This is a semi-detached house, so it's probably just creaking or sound carrying through from next door".

However, as they sat there chatting, he looked over at a noise from the conservatory which was attached to the lounge and separated from it by a glass panel door. Although there was obviously no-one in the conservatory, as plain as day he saw the door handle push itself down and the door swing open by about ten inches.

He told his friend what he had just seen, and he went into the conservatory and checked that there were no windows or exterior doors open anywhere that could have made a through draught open the door. There was nothing.

The two of them felt "freaked out" for the rest of the evening and remained sitting on the sofa, not daring to go anywhere else for hours - because the incident had left such an eerie feeling. He says the sight of that handle untouched by human hand and yet clearly being moved downwards still plays on his mind today.

SUTTON CUM LOUND,

Nottinghamshire

A gentleman wrote in to tell me about the very unpleasant experience he and his wife had whilst living in a property in this tiny village in Nottinghamshire.

The events happened between 1998 and 1999 when they rented a small cottage from his Aunt, and can probably best be described as a classic poltergeist haunting. Several members of their family experienced things, as well as friends who visited. Eventually, they asked the local vicar in and asked him to bless the house to try and rid themselves of it.

They also asked a well-known ghost hunter to come round and rid the house of the spirit. He told them that actually, there was more than one. The first was a young man who had died in the 1700s when he had accidentally fallen off a haystack and landed on a pitchfork. His ghost was restless and, they were told, did not want to believe he had died over a stupid accident whilst showing off to his mates. The second was the spirit of a musician, who had been drawn to their cottage because their own son played the drums. The spirit had not "passed over", apparently, because he thought he was just having a bad drug trip, and did not realise that a drug overdose had in fact killed him!

They later found out that the previous occupant, a very old lady, had tried to tell her carers that the place was haunted, but they had brushed it off as the imaginings of the elderly. Then, after her death and builders came in to renovate the cottage, they too were plagued by ghostly happenings.

Some of the things that occurred over those eventful couple of years were the frequent popping of lightbulbs, and glasses of wine which would suddenly lunch themselves across the room.

On at least one occasion, they came into the living room to find that all of the CDs had been taken out of their protective plastic cases and spread out all over the floor.

The doors would often slam with no apparent cause, and the kettle would turn itself off or on at will. There would be orbs of light seen by the naked eye, and on a couple of occasions they saw static electricity run across the ceiling as an arcing blue light. (I saw this once inside a car - and it is honestly a very unnerving thing to see!)

Sometimes, when sleeping in the house, people would be awoken in the dead of night by the sensation of a heavy weight sitting down on top of them.

Pictures hanging on the walls would fly off their hooks, and the sound of footsteps was frequently heard - along with an unpleasant groaning sound.

On another occasion, a child's yo-yo was thrown across the room, and at other times the sound of stones grinding together would sound loudly all over the cottage.

My witness said that sometimes it felt like his hair was literally standing on end with fright for weeks at a time.

Eventually they put the cottage up for sale, but some of the people who came to view it said they could sense something unpleasant about the place. On one occasion, a Romany gypsy came to the door selling lucky heather and clothes pegs. As soon as our witness answered the door, the Gypsy told him the place felt cursed, and that she would not set foot in it. She lost all interest in selling her heather and left, saying that they should pack up their belongings and do the same!

My witness told me that up until the time he lived in this house he had never believed in the supernatural, so this was all quite a culture shock for him.

In his own words, he said that the funniest thing that happened was when a friend of theirs and his fiancé stayed with them for the night. He explained, "We sat in the kitchen eating breakfast. My friend, (who worked as a locum pharmacist) was discussing his inability to sleep after he was awoken by the weight of the spirit sitting on his legs in the night. He recalled sitting upright and witnessing blue static electricity moving around the bedroom ceiling. As he finished telling us this I asked whether anybody like a fresh cup of tea? Right on cue the kettle switched itself on and began to boil! Needless to say my friend and his partner left very rapidly after that!"

TEMPLE BRUER, Knights Templar Tower, Lincolnshire

A gentleman wrote to tell me his thoughts about Temple Bruer. He said that it is a strange place, and a couple of slightly odd things have happened to him there over the years. The tower is one of the last remaining buildings of the Knights Templar still standing in Britain today. Now standing within a farm yard, it is a brooding looking building which was in use between 1150 and 1312a.d. Its name comes from a corruption of the French word for heather - since at the time it was in use it would have been in the middle of a desolate, heather-covered heathland.

He explained, "I was working near the preceptory clearing fallen trees that had come down over the track during the bad storms we had 4 or 5 years ago, probably in around 2014 or so. I was there all day without issue, then as it started to get dark I had a real strong feeling of dread come over me which I just had no explanation for. I began to feel very distinctly that I was being watched from the tower.

"It was properly dark when I finished and I just wanted to get out of there. I packed all my tools away in quite a hurry, and jumped in the van. However, I then discovered that the van battery was absolutely dead. Luckily a chap I knew was working in one of the buildings up the road and he came and jump started the van for me. It was weird, because it was the one and only time I had trouble with the battery like that."

He went on to say that on another occasion, he and his wife were out having a little day out together, and drove past Temple Bruer. Just near the airfield, they saw the quaint old church and decided to have a walk around it. They spotted a small car park just close to the church, with neatly mown grass and a white chain link fence around it.

They parked their car, and walked the few yards along the roadside to the church itself. They had a pleasant time walking about, then returned to the car and left.

A couple of years later they thought they might visit the church again as they happened to be in the area. They found the church again with no problem – exactly where they expected it to be.

Of the little car park, however, no sign. At all. Not even a now disused area where it might once have been – the hedges on both sides of the road for some distance either side of the church were clearly well established and well grown, and permitted absolutely no room whatsoever for there to have been a car park...

Another lady told me that since she works for Heritage Lincolnshire, she has spent many hours on her own in Temple Bruer tower working – but has never in all that time seen or heard anything unusual. She said that despite her own lack of experiences, she had heard of many people who had seen things around there.

It is said that the lanes all around the building are haunted – and that people see the figures of men wearing the white tabard associated with the Knights run across the road or run through the hedges at the side.

TOTTERIDGE COMMON, North London

One witness wrote to tell me about a particularly creepy thing that happened when he and his wife were out walking with their young son on Totteridge Common one day.

Their son was about five years old at the time, and so the family was wandering along at a child's pace just enjoying their afternoon stroll. They were making their way along an old bridleway which runs from just across from where Totteridge Common, St Andrew's Church stands, across the side of the common and over Folly Brook.

Chattering away as small children do, their little son suddenly asked, out of nowhere, "Mummy, why are the men in funny uniforms lying under the ground here?" He was looking down at his feet with a puzzled expression on his face.

The adults made light of it, but inside they were feeling distinctly creepy!

Interestingly, St Andrew's Church boasts a Yew Tree in its grounds which is at least 1,000 years old – and quite possibly as old as 2,000 years, according to experts from Kew Gardens. The church also appears to have been built on a much older, possibly pagan circular site.

TWICKENHAM, South West London – AMYAND PARK ROAD

I came across a report that prior to 1964, a row of small terraced houses in Amyand Park Road, Twickenham, were haunted by the ghost of a small boy, before the houses were demolished to make way for the building of a new supermarket.

Curious, I wrote out locally to see if anyone knew which supermarket this was and whether it was haunted. As is my custom, and so as not to give a bias to any witnesses who chose to come forward and give me their own accounts, I did not specify the nature of the haunting.

The request sparked a very lively debate about which part of Amyand Park Road I might be talking about, with people swapping memories about various old shops and local characters that had come and gone over the intervening decades.

Eventually, the chatter and banter back and forth decided that the most likely site I was describing was the area where Waitrose Supermarket now stands. Over the years, it has been owned by various supermarket chains. Technically it's not quite on Amyand Park Road, but right next to the end of it, and opposite the delightfully named Cabbage Patch Pub.

General consensus was that the building Waitrose currently occupies was built slightly before 1970 - which would tie in quite well with the source story I had found. One lady particularly remembered the cottages being there, because her grandmother had lived in one of them at one time.

One gentleman was able to recall that where the supermarket and its car park now stand, there used to be large houses and shops on London Road, semi-detached houses on Amyand Park Road, and terraces houses on both Arragon Road and Katherine Road. He said that after the developers had left them all empty for a number of years they began to look a bit run down until squatters moved in. The authorities then moved in, evicted the squatters and ripped the floorboards out of all the houses - leaving them looking really grim before finally being demolished to make way for the supermarket.

And amazingly, one person wrote in to say that she had been told that the Waitrose supermarket itself is now haunted by the ghost of a little boy who is seen running up and down the aisles. Sadly she had never actually seen the ghost herself.

Another lady described how her elderly aunt used to work in the area around the Cabbage Patch, and she remembers seeing the children from St Mary's School walking along crocodile fashion on their way to the train station to be evacuated during World War II. I can't help but wonder if there is any connection between this and the haunting. Maybe one of the evacuees died, and returned to his old home in spirit?

UPPER CALDECOTE, Bedfordshire

Upper Caldecote is a small village which lies not far to the west of Biggleswade, near the A1 Great North Road in Bedfordshire. One lady wrote to tell me about her experience with a Ouija board whilst living in a house there.

A Ouija board is a device used for contacting spirits of the dead. Pronounced "Wee-jee" by most people, apparently the name derives from the French and German words for "Yes" - "oui" and "ja". The boards first appeared in the 1890s in America, and were sold as mysterious novelty "games". They are traditionally a wooden board which can be laid upon a desktop, and which have the letters of the alphabet arranged in a semicircle , along with the words "hello" "goodbye" "yes, and "no" painted in the corners. There is a small, usually teardrop shaped planchette, upon which the sitters can place their fingers. The planchette is designed to glide easily across the surface of the board, and the idea is that spirit uses the energy of the people lightly resting their fingertips upon it to race the planchette across the board pointing to letters to spell out messages from "the other side".

Many people believe them to be a harmless bit of fun. Many more believe it to be a reliable tool to use to speak to the spirits of their deceased loved ones. And quite a few believe them to be inherently evil and dangerous to use.

My correspondent told me that when she was around 12 years old, in the early 1990s, she and a school friend were having a sleepover at her house. They decided to create their own Ouija board out of paper and made their own little pointer to act as the planchette. To prepare for their experiment, they excitedly and surreptitiously collected a few stones from the nearby graveyard to place around their "board" and give it the necessary "creepy factor".

They couldn't wait for it to be officially time to retire to the bedroom, and as soon as they were safely ensconced in the cosy room, they set up their board and tentatively placed their fingers on the pointer - asking question after question and hoping for an answer.

After a while, when absolutely nothing had happened, they grew bored with their game, and pushed the whole thing out of the way under the camp bed that had been set up for her friend to sleep on.

They busied themselves with other amusements until late in the evening, when suddenly they realised they could hear a weird noise emanating from under the camp bed. Listening closely, they thought it sounded like paper rustling as it moved over other paper.

Kneeling down, they peered at the board under the bed – and saw immediately that everything on it had been moved around from how they had left it. Scared, they retrieved it from under the bed, and threw all of the stones out of the bedroom window, then screwed up what remained of their paper "board" and threw it in the bin.

A bit rattled by the experience, they settled down into bed after a while, and chatted themselves into a sleepy, drowsy state. It didn't last long, because every time they drifted off, they would be awoken by the sound of something or someone knocking on the bedroom window – as if something were asking to be let in.

They spent a fretful, scared night, disturbed a number of times by the knocks at the window. Eventually, to their relief, it was time to get up and start a new day – but the expected relief from their night time fright didn't come.

As they moved around the house for the rest of that day, the knocks would sound on the window of whichever room they happened to be in – as if something was following them and watching them. Eventually, as the evening drew in, the hateful sounds finally faded away and were heard no more.

Suffice to say – she has never touched a Ouija board since!

Their house was an old house, and it had a few surprises of its own even without their "help" with the Ouija board. Over the years, lights would mysteriously turn themselves on or off, and sometimes there was the sound of kitchen chairs being dragged across the old quarry tiles in the kitchen late at night when everyone was asleep in bed.

UTTERBY, Lincolnshire

This next story was actually sent to me in response to my research questions for my previous book "The Roadmap of British Ghosts", but unfortunately missed the deadline to get included – so here it is now instead.

A lady wrote to explain that sometime around either 1996 or 1997, her ex-husband was driving home from his late shift in Immingham, Lincolnshire.

He was driving along the A16, and had not long passed the turning for Ludborough on his left and was coming towards Utterby – travelling quite fast because at that time in the morning the roads were completely devoid of any other traffic.

Suddenly, someone or something in the back seat of his car pushed really hard on the back of his driver's seat – twice. Both times, the push was hard enough and sure enough to rock him forward in the seat. He knew full well that he was alone in the car, and was not surprisingly suddenly terrified as to what might be "back there".

Realising that he had two choices – carry on and get home to light and safety, or stop and get out of the car in the lonely, dark countryside, he made the only sensible choice. He adjusted the rearview mirror so that he could not see behind himself anymore, and carried on – playing music to distract himself. (I had to chuckle when I read that – you'd be amazed at how many times I did that myself whilst researching for "Roadmap"!)

When he got home and spoke to his wife, he was really shaken up by the experience.

WARMINSTER, Wiltshire – BOREHAM ROAD

One witness told me about her experience at an address in Boreham Road, Warminster in 1991. She was only quite young at the time, in her early twenties, and had a boyfriend who lived in the property, which is a terraced house with a narrow frontage enclosed by iron railings.

They had been seeing each other for a couple of years, and sometimes she would stay over at his house. She would often do little jobs around the house for him, and one day the job she was doing was painting one of the bedrooms.

She had the radio blaring away on her favourite music station, and as painting and decorating was something she really enjoyed, she was happily just finishing the walls and making a start on glossing the door.

She is not particularly tall in stature, so had to use a little stool step to stand on in order to reach the top of the door. She had closed the door, and pushed the stool right up against it in order to reach the area she was working on.

Something caught her attention whilst she was up on the stool painting away, and she looked down at the handle and sliding bolt of the door. As she watched – the sliding bolt lifted itself to the "slide" position, and then moved into the "locked" position.

Thoroughly spooked by what she had just seen, she climbed down off the stool and put her paintbrush into the tin of turpentine. She tried the handle and confirmed that she was right – the door had firmly bolted itself, shutting her in the room. Terrified, she quickly unbolted the door and ran out of the house – waiting outside until her boyfriend came home.

On another occasion, she had stayed overnight, and they had gone to bed fairly early since her boyfriend had work the next day and would need to leave at about 5am. At around 2.30am, she awoke from her slumber needing to use the toilet. Tiptoeing quietly out of bed and across the landing, she made use of the facilities and then quietly started her short journey back to the warm bed.

As she crossed the landing, she distinctly heard a male voice call her name and say "Goodnight!" Too startled to think about it, she automatically replied "Goodnight" – and scurried back across the landing and into bed next to her still snoring boyfriend.

WARWICK, Warwickshire – ST JOHNS HOUSE MUSEUM

St Johns House Museum, in the heart of Warwick, is a stunning old building which boasts 900 years of history. It has seen various roles over the years – as a house, a hospital, a school, and now a civic building as it is operated as a museum by the local council. It is also a very popular location for ghost tours, and you can book with various companies to go on a late night ghost hunt there.

My friend and I booked for an evening there with one such company (Paranormal Eye UK) in 2016. We had a great time, and a couple of interesting things happened which I can't quite explain. The first was when I did a lone vigil in a room full of children's toys. The rest of my group were in the next room over, trying their hand at a Ouija board, which I had preferred not to take part in. The rooms were separated by an open doorway, so I could clearly hear what they were saying, and also had some small amounts of light spilling into the room I was in from the very dim torch they were using to see the letters on their board.

I sat listening to the chatter from next door, and acclimating myself to being able to tell which moving shadows in my room were being caused by the slight light spillage from their activity next door. After a while, I was sure that as well as their shadows, I was occasionally seeing the shadow of a cat move about the room. It was stalking along with its back slightly arched and its tail held up straight in the air, and it would move a few feet each time before fading out of view.

After a while, my vigil came to an end because the Ouija Board next door had tried to fling itself on the floor when they asked it if anyone wanted to speak to Ruth who was sitting in the room next door..

Later in the evening, myself, my friend, one other guest and the organiser of the events did a vigil with just the four of us in the Old School Room. It is high ceilinged squarish room, with dark wood panelling on the walls. On full wall is actually a bi-folding old wooden and glass door which enables the room to be enlarged by including the room next door, which has glass museum display cabinets arranged in it.

Inside the school room are memorabilia from the building's time as a school, including rows of school benches and the teacher's imposing carved wooden chair and dais. The four of us were sitting around one of the wooden benches, and we the three guests were attempting a Ouija board. The organiser was not touching the board as they have a policy not to - they allow the guests to experience anything on their own. There was not much activity on the board - it was kind of shuffling around a little bit without any real intent.

Suddenly, when we asked it a question, there was an extremely loud, and somewhat irritated sounding bang - from directly underneath the bench we were using as a table for the board. It was so loud, and strong, that it shook the bench and we all felt it.

Our host immediately radioed her colleagues elsewhere in the building to see if anyone had inadvertently made the noise - particularly the group that were in the cellar, maybe. They all radioed back to say no, nothing, and in fact no-one was currently in the cellar below us.

Even as she spoke, there was another resounding bang on the partition door behind where she was sitting - followed immediately by another one on the wall opposite on the wood panelling. We had no explanation for the loud sounds (much louder than just settling creaks and groans that buildings make).

Later still, at the very end of the night, we were again given lone vigil time. It was somewhere around 2am by this time, and I persuaded my friend to come back into the toy room with me to see if I could see the cat shadow again. We sat ourselves on the padded lid of a child's toy bench, with our backs to a small window and facing the door into the room in the far right corner.

We sat silently for maybe ten minutes or so, listening to the fading sounds of the others elsewhere in the building as they too settled themselves quietly down to wait. We were in almost pitch darkness, and our room was quiet and still. I was concentrating hard on the floor, waiting to see if I could determine the cat shadow again, or else debunk it as something natural.

Suddenly, something blew hard directly into my left ear, and a piece of wispy gauze like cloth blew across the corner of my face - like maybe a piece of net curtain, or a piece of lace.

Startled, I grabbed my friend's knee and whispered - "Did you hear that?" She didn't answer, though - but instead screamed, jumped up, and headed for the door at high speed - accidentally dislodging her Iphone which went skittering off across the floor.

Now I am disabled, and walk with a stick - very slowly - so there was no way I could run after her, and neither was I willing to be left alone with whatever it was that had made her scream. As she jumped up and started to flee, I grabbed the trailing end of her scarf and yanked her to a standstill - furiously whispering "don't leave me!"

I made her wait while we turned on a torch, retrieved her poor Iphone (thankfully undamaged) and then made a more dignified exit from the building into the carpark, where we burst out laughing and shared a shaky cigarette. I was dying to know what she had experienced which made her flee - but her reply was, "Nothing! I just knew if you were grabbing my knee something was happening and I wasn't waiting to find out!" I'm pleased to say in the three years since she and I have ghost hunted a lot together - and she is now really good at marching straight at whatever is occurring to see if she can experience it or debunk it, but her reaction that day still makes us cry with laughter.

At the very end of the night, when all the building lights were turned back on and we were getting ready to leave, I slipped quickly back into the toy room to see which piece of material had blown across my face and whether it might just have been caused by a draught.

There was no material anywhere in the room. The small window behind where we had been sitting was literally rusted and painted shut - it clearly had not been opened in many years. It was covered by a stiff, shiny plastic feeling roller blind.

I later asked whether anyone else had experienced anything in the building. A lady wrote to me to tell me of her own experience - again on one of the many ghost hunting evenings that can be booked there. This was in 2017, and although she didn't see or hear anything, the Ouija board her group were using kept spelling out her daughter's name - who is alive and well. And most curiously, her daughter had a school trip booked to visit the museum the following week...

The night after her ghost hunt at the museum, she was woken in the middle of the night by a sound. Her glasses, which she had of course taken off when she retired, had a broken lens. She propped them up on a shelf, and settled back to sleep. A while later she was awoken again, and this time the glasses had moved to the middle of the room, and one of the lenses had popped out and was found lying on the floor on the far side of the room.

WELLS, Somerset - THE SWAN

I found an account from 1978 that a pub called The King Charles Parlour on the High Street in this historic old town was haunted by the ghost of a cavalier from the English Civil War. The King Charles Parlour ceased trading as a pub, and as far as I could tell the building was now possibly occupied by a travel agents shop.

The original account said the ghost was often seen on the stairway of the pub, which dates back to the Jacobean period. There has also been the sound of a harpsichord reported, and the feeling of someone brushing past in the hallway.

Curious as to whether the haunting was still continuing despite the change of building occupancy, I asked for people's own accounts.

One person explained to me that there is an alleyway next to the travel agents, which led to a square where The Kings Parlour used to be, and then carried on to the White Hart pub. This alleyway looks to go beneath the Star Hotel, and go past the back of The Swan hotel to the back of the White Hart.

One lady told me that she worked in The Swan in 2017 as a chambermaid, and on one occasion she was cleaning one of the rooms, and made the bed with fresh sheets as part of her duties. She turned away for a moment, and when she turned back, one of the bed's corners had been disturbed and the sheets flung up.

Assuming she must have caught it somehow and pulled it, she sighed and remade it. Twice more, she turned around to find the same corner mussed up and had to remake it, before she could finally leave the room.

Someone else wrote to say that she had worked in the building during the mid-1990s when it was a gentleman's outfitters shop. The building, she said, had three floors but they really only used two of them. The top floor was left largely untouched and the rooms still had hotel numbers on their doors and basins in each one. She had been told that a cavalier soldier had been killed during a fight on the stairwell, and that the building was haunted by his ghost. She said that the upper floor had a very strange feeling about it.

Another person told me that in around 2006 she worked in the shop next door to the travel agents, which was actually part of the same building. She described herself as a non-believer in the supernatural - until she worked in that shop. She described how all of the employees would experience moving shadows where none should be, and strange whispering sounds that seemed to be straight into your ear. Sometimes the whisper would clearly be your own name.

She explained that the worst affected area of the building was the second floor back room and anywhere on the top floor. Once, a colleague and her followed a lady into one of the back rooms on the second floor – only to find the mysterious lady had disappeared. My witness had also heard that a customer's child had once asked about the man with the big hat he had seen walking down the stairs.

On some occasions, items would fly off the shelves even though no-one had touched them, and sometimes they would open up in the morning to find that things had been moved around.

Another lady told me that the White Hart was also haunted, and that it had poltergeist activity in one room in particular, where things would literally launch themselves across the room.

Several other people also came forward to mention a number of other shops along the High Street and the ghostly activity they experience in them, so it would seem the entire area is quite active.

WELWYN, DIGSWELL and OAKLANDS, Hertfordshire

As I explained in the prologue to this book, I got some interesting responses about the general area when I tried to ascertain whether my old childhood home (which was the place which sparked my abiding interest in the paranormal) was still showing signs of being haunted all these years later.

One witness remembered that her parents had been in Hertfordshire, driving down an old narrow lane at night, when the misty form of a man wearing an old style long riding coat walked across the road in the headlights of their car.

Another had a friend who many years ago was a train driver. He was driving a very late train one night and had to cross the Digswell Viaduct. Also sometimes called The Welwyn Viaduct, this beautiful piece of architecture carries the trains over the River Mimram and its shallow valley. It was designed by William Cubbit, and opened by Queen Victoria on 6 August 1850. There is a tale that she was frightened of the height of it and refused to actually travel over it.

Our train driver did not believe in ghosts. But on this night, he saw several people in old fashioned clothes standing on the viaduct itself (where today pedestrians are absolutely not able to access) as his train thundered through.

Another lady said that her house in Mardley Hill (part of Oaklands) was haunted when she was growing up. The ghost was that of a small boy aged around seven years old or so, whom they used to refer to as "George". She first remembers seeing him a couple of years after they moved into the house, in around 1973. He would visit them in their bedrooms at night because he wanted to play – especially with her brothers whom he was obviously drawn to as possible playmates. He would sit on the end of their beds and wait until his presence woke them up – and he seemed especially fond of her youngest brother.

She said she herself only ever saw him at night, but the youngest sibling would see him more often and would even ask their mother to set a place at the tea table for "George". Her mother recalls that the children would often talk about "George", but never saw him herself.

However, sometimes their mother would ask them if they had been up during the night, because she herself had been woken by the sounds of sirens or bells on the various toy fire engines and police cars her brothers had, which were down in their playroom. None of the children had in fact been up during the night – so who was turning the toys on and playing with them?

On other occasions, the sound of someone playing their piano would disturb the family when they were all together in the lounge. The piano was also in the playroom.

She described "George" as a happy ghost, and does not seem to have ever felt threatened by or scared of his friendly presence. The family dogs would react as if they could see him, and sometimes act as if someone was petting them.

When their grandparents came to stay, her grandmother would not sleep in the playroom (which doubled up as a guest room), because she complained that she would be woken up by the feeling of someone gently patting her....

She also recalled that another house in their street also had a ghost, but wasn't able to give much detail about that one.

Another person told me that the lane towards Datchworth was haunted by the sound of a ghostly horse and cart clip clopping along it - and they themselves had once heard this visitation. The legend I had found for one of my previous books relating to this area of lanes related to a horse and carriage, so that was interesting as a possible correlation.

WESTBURY, Wiltshire

One of my correspondents told me about the house which she currently resides in. It is in the tiny village of Westbury in Wiltshire, a place perhaps most famous because it boasts one of the amazing and ancient white chalk figures of England: the Westbury Horse.

She and her husband moved into the property on 16th September 2013. They were excited about getting their new home, and finally got the call in the afternoon that they could now collect the keys.

They loaded their car with as much as they could fit in it, drove to collect the keys, then on to the new house. Two more trips and all their belongings were in - and although they only had a mattress on the floor to sleep on that first night, they were so happy and excited with their new home that they celebrated with a bottle of champagne, sitting in their makeshift bed on the floor.

She had tuned their radio into a radio station called "Breeze" as they liked the choice of music that was playing, and they were happily making plans. Before long, they had finished their bottle of champagne and decided to go downstairs and fetch a second one. As they went through the rooms on the ground floor, they noticed a cat looking in at them through the French doors into their garden. They stopped to fuss the feline for a few minutes, then eventually grabbed their second bottle and made their way back up the stairs.

The radio was no longer playing music – even though neither of them had touched it when they left the room a few minutes earlier. On checking, she found that it was now tuned to Medium Wave, instead of FM Stereo, where it had been. She straight away knew that there was something else in the house with them, but said nothing as her husband does not like any talk of the paranormal – finding it too scary to contemplate. Part of her conviction came from the fact that she could feel that the house was colder inside than it was outside in the garden.

Her husband works night shifts on the railways, and he returned to work on the night of 17th September. This meant our witness was alone at night, but it is a pattern they were used to and it never bothered her. This first night that he left for work from their new home, his van was parked quite close to their front door, so she stood in the doorway to wave him off. As she waited for him to climb in and start the van, she glanced over her shoulder back towards their kitchen.

She could clearly see the shadow of a man standing in the kitchen doorway – even though her husband was still warming the van up and definitely not in the house. She didn't say anything or react – she didn't want to upset her husband, and having experienced the paranormal in previous properties in her life, she knew she was not going to feel afraid herself.

When she looked back after her husband set off, the shadow man was gone, and she calmly took herself off to bed where she spent a quiet and undisturbed night.

Over the next few weeks, the activity in the house started to pick up. Sometimes during the day, when her husband was sleeping after his night shift, she would hear footsteps stomping around the house, especially upstairs. Just to be sure, a couple of times she crept quietly upstairs and made sure that her husband was in fact still snoring peacefully in bed - so clearly it was not him making the noise.

At other times, doors would rattle in their frames as if someone was trying to open them, or sharp bangs would sound from a part of the house where no-one living was present to have caused them. It was noticeable that at night, just as her husband left for work, there would be a couple of sharp bangs on the bedroom floor as if someone was trying to get her attention.

One night, she took a shower in their ensuite bathroom, then settled in bed to watch the T.V they had recently installed in the room. At some point, warm and comfortable, she drifted off to sleep, but was woken at around 1.30am by her phone ringing. Waking, she answered it, and it was her husband who was on his shift break. They chatted for a while, as they often did, but whilst talking she noticed a flash of light coming from their ensuite bathroom.

She looked over, and saw the same shadow man she had seen when they first moved in standing there. She described him as tall - and weirdly the flash of light which had caught her attention seemed to be like a bolt of lightning coming out of the top of his head. She was so astonished at the sight that she fell silent - even though her husband was waiting for her to speak on the other end of the phone. The shadow man stayed for maybe a minute - before there was a flash of something akin to sheet lightning, and he disappeared.

This time she had to tell her husband what had just happened, because obviously he was worried about why she had suddenly gone silent. He took it quite well, but they stayed on the phone together for quite some time afterwards.

From then on, she would often see a shadow man standing at the top of her stairs looking down at her - but she was never sure if the shadows were of the same man she had seen the first time in the kitchen, or of different men. She figured that they weren't doing her any harm or bothering her, so she would just carry on with whatever she was doing at the time and ignore them.

Then one day, she had been out to fetch some shopping, and came back in through her front door with her bags. As both hands were full, she momentarily stopped and put them on the floor in the hallway, so that she could turn and close the front door behind her.

As she went to straighten up, she could suddenly see a full figure of a man in her lounge. He was a little taller than her (she is 5'2"), so not particularly tall for a man, had mousey brown hair, and was wearing a light coloured shirt with a brown waistcoat over it.

She later found out from a neighbour that one of the previous owners of the house had died there – and his description matched that of the figure she saw that day in her lounge.

WEST PECKHAM, Kent

One witness who wrote to me particularly fascinated me, because she opened her correspondence with, "Hi there. I need to write to you right this minute because she is here!"

The "she" in question was of course their resident ghost. My witness went on to explain that they live in a cottage that for the most part dates back to the 15th Century, but it is recorded that their inglenook dates back to 1210a.d. An inglenook is a recess next to a fireplace, and so an inglenook fireplace is one which deliberately had these recesses built in – they were used for warming oneself or clothing etc. The fireplace in this particular building would have been part of an earlier byre or cattle shed, with a primitive dwelling incorporated.

Next to their front door there is still the old well, which once upon a time supplied the hamlet of West Peckham with water. At one point in its long history, it was cared for by an old lady, who would keep the well free of contamination and clear of overgrowth etc.

It is the ghost of this old lady who is still frequently sensed or seen around their cottage. She is usually either around the well itself, or in the oldest part of the house. My correspondent explained that there is nothing frightening about their ghost – she seems to carry with her a happy and calm demeanour. The couple are busy renovating the old property and especially its grounds, which over time had become very neglected.

The ghost is very short, and is always dressed in dark brown. She seems to move very quickly, and sometimes when they are out working in the garden they see her darting about inside the house. If they happen to be inside when she visits, the temperature in the room noticeably drops when she passes near.

Usually it is just the couple themselves who see her, but recently their landlord came to visit and saw her in the oldest part of the house.

And at the time my witness was writing to me, the whole right side of her body was standing up in goosebumps – which she tells me is a sure sign that the ghost was present in the room.

WHALEY BRIDGE, Derbyshire

In around 1981 or so, when the lady who wrote to tell me of her ghost experience was around 18 years old, she was walking along Old Road in Whaley Bridge in the High Peak district of Derbyshire.

It was dusk as she walked, but she could see an old man standing in part of the road which seemed to be cobbled with overhanging trees. He was clearly wearing a tall top hat and was carrying a fancy looking cane in one hand. He was only there for a few seconds, and when she looked again, he had disappeared and the road no longer looked as if it was cobbled.

She spoke to her own grandfather about what she had seen – puzzled by how the man had seemed to be there one minute and not the next, and how the road had seemed briefly changed.

He told her that there used to be an undertaker's establishment just along that stretch of Old Road. The horses and carriages were kept just along there – and yes, the road used to be cobbled. In those days, the trees did overhang the road more, he explained, because there weren't all the tall lorries and vans which they would be cut back to accommodate nowadays. The undertaker used to perform the solemn duty of walking along in front of the horse drawn hearse in his top hat and suit, paying respects to the dead as they were taken to their final resting place.

Curiously, another lady wrote to say that in the early 1970s she used to have a paper round on Old Road. She would deliver the papers very early in the morning – usually before 7am, and in the summertime it was quite pleasant to be out so early in the bright, cool morning sunshine. She explained that one summer morning, just after 6am, she was coming down the path from The Manse, and there was a man on the footpath.

In her words, "I said hello and he just carried on walking. He had really old fashioned clothes and a big tall hat. I turned round to see where he went and he had disappeared."

It seems likely the undertaker's ghost was active for at least a number of decades from his death until at least the 1980s.

There is a road which branches off from Old Road called Bings Road, and this piece of road apparently also boasts a haunted well. Some correspondents told me that nearby Bings Wood had the ghost of a man with no face, and it is possibly him who haunted the well. The well itself is described as a stone trough tucked into the bank, and a couple of people mentioned that it felt creepy to walk past, especially at night.

One person had heard an old tale that many years ago a young girl was knocked down and killed when a cart became detached from the horse who was pulling it on the steep part of Bings Road, and careened down to the junction with Old Road, where the unfortunate lass was struck and killed. The story is that her ghost now haunts the road.

One gentleman told me about quite an unnerving encounter he had at his mother's house in Whaley Bridge. He was about 15 years old at the time, and happened to be home alone one winter's night at about 6 or 7pm in the evening. It was an unpleasant night with a cold, gusty wind, but he knew their family dog Toddy needed to toilet, so he had put him out in the garden on a long chain (there was always a risk he'd go wandering if left untethered!).

After a while, the dog started barking, so he got up to go and let him back into the house. Stepping outside, he realised that the wind had blown loose the door to the electricity box, and it was now banging back and forth on its hinges. He thought he had better wedge the door shut using one of the wheelie bins nearby, in case the wind picked up even more strongly and caused damage to it.

As he walked towards the box, he happened to glance up the garden towards where the garage was. He suddenly realised that he could see someone sitting propped up against their garage wall with their legs extended out in front of them - and it was this figure that Toddy was busy barking at.

His first thought was that this must be someone who was drunk and had been trying to take a shortcut by hopping over their wall. Thinking that he ought to both check they were OK on this cold, stormy night, but also send them on their way, he started to walk towards the figure. As he got closer, he could clearly see that it was a man, as he had first suspected, and that the man was wearing what looked like it might be a tuxedo.

His brain was busy scrambling to come up with a plausible reason for all of this - a fancy dress party maybe? Drunk? But at the same time, realisation was dawning that as it was only 7pm in the evening, who on earth would be leaving a party already drunk at that early time?

The worry was also starting to set in that in reality, he himself was only a lad of 15 and he was going to have to try and rouse and move on a grown man, who may or may not have been drinking. His concern grew exponentially as he approached, because when he was only about six feet away from the figure, the man raised his hands, which were covered in pristine white gloves – and started rhythmically waving his arms about – a bit like he was conducting an orchestra!

Slowing a bit at the weird antics, our witness peered at the man's face from about six feet away, hoping that maybe he would recognise who it was and that would make the encounter go a bit easier.

His concern turned to terror quite quickly, because he realised with a jolt that he could not make out any features on the man's face. Although he could perfectly clearly see the man's tuxedo, white gloves, and now even bow tie – it was as if some shadow was cast over his face obscuring everything there. And weirdly, he was also totally silent – whereas you might expect a drunk who thought he was conducting an orchestra to be either singing along or maybe belching!

Our witness tried to say something like, "get out of the garden, mate" but found that his voice was completely paralysed, he was sweating with fear and his hair was standing on end – accompanied by a horrible prickly feeling of something ***really not right*** about this whole weird situation, even as his brain was frantically trying to rationalise away what he was looking at.

In the end, he back slowly away, then turned, grabbed his dog and freed him from the chain, and dashed back into the house. As he turned to shut the door behind him he could see that the person was still sitting there. He locked the door behind him, and when his Mum came home a little while later, she found her terrified son sitting in the chair facing the garden door and clutching a hammer.

He says that to this day, he cannot say for sure that this was something supernatural – but the whole episode was just weird and he is well aware of how his body was reacting as if he was facing something dangerous that he should get away from.

WHITTON, South West London – NELSON ROAD

A witness told me about her experience in this outer borough of London. It was a few years ago, and she was driving one sunny Sunday afternoon from Hanworth down Nelson Road towards Hospital Bridge Road. She had her daughters in the car with her, and they were on their way to have a nice family Sunday lunch with her own parents.

She had just driven over the railway bridge and was approaching the zebra crossing near the little parade of shops next to the turning for Whitton Way. At the side of the road, waiting to use the zebra crossing, was a lady pushing a pram.

She doesn't particularly recall anything memorable about the lady herself, just that she was wearing some sort of dark coloured coat, but specifically remembers the pram, because it was that which caught her attention. It was an old style Silver Cross pram of the sort which was popular in the 1950s or so, and which in this day and age you just never see except in T.V. shows or museums.

She stopped her car to allow the lady to cross the pedestrian crossing at the same time as a car coming from the opposite direction also stopped, and turned her head to speak to her daughters in the back seat and point out the unusual old pram to them – particularly as it reminded her of the one her own parents used to have for her own baby sister – the girls' aunt.

After a couple of seconds, she realised no-one had crossed the road, and turned her head fully back around to the front – to realise that there was no sign of the lady or her pram anywhere! It was so puzzling, since there was nowhere for her to have gone out of sight so quickly, that both she and the other driver (also a lady) actually got out of their cars and looked around in bewilderment, asking each other – "Where did she go?" "Did you see her?"

In the end she had to just shrug it off and continue the journey, even though both daughters confirmed that they too had seen the lady waiting to cross, and had looked at the pram their mother was pointing out. They said they were watching her all the time, and she had just disappeared into thin air.

My witness still lives in the area and frequently drives that same stretch of road, but has never seen anything else odd along there.

WOODSTOCK, Oxfordshire - THE MACDONALD BEAR HOTEL

Parts of this beautiful looking old hotel were built over 900 years ago, so it's perhaps not surprising with all that history that something sometimes goes bump in the night...

Originally a coaching inn built in the 1200s, it is supposed to have a number of hauntings which manifest - including disembodied footsteps, the spectre of a young boy, the ghost of a workman who fell from the roof a couple of hundred years ago, and the sound of crying which emanates from one of the bedrooms.

One witness told me that he worked there for 3 years from June 2014 to Sept 2017. He worked the breakfast shift, and so would arrive to start work at 6am. Quite often, as they hurried in to start their shift, he would see something running down the hall just ahead of them that would be glimpsed for a second before disappearing.

They would often experience plates or glasses mysteriously falling off the tables, and on one occasion a heavy decanter full of orange juice seemed to get mysteriously pushed off the table even though no-one was actually near it.

On other occasions, as he was busy using the Henry Hoover, the device would get unplugged from the wall - just as if some childish ghost were playing pranks. Once, he went down to the basement which was used as a store room to fetch something, and while he was down there all the lights went out and the door slammed!

Sometimes during those years, guests would speak to the staff about their own experiences during the night – like waking up to find a scratch they had no explanation for, to seeing the reflection of someone in the mirror. Some guests woke up to find the furniture in the room had moved – and in one particular room a rocking chair would start rocking in the middle of the night.

Another witness told me that she used to work as a chambermaid there when she was in her late teens. She was told then that Room 16 was haunted, so whenever she had to work in there she refused to have the door shut – because she always felt like something was watching her.

Someone else mentioned that when another author stayed overnight there, he was so tired the next day because he had been woken up by the sound of the furniture in his room moving about.

One lady told me that when her mother worked in the restaurant, there was a note on the menu for the restaurant which said that the Hotel was already ancient when nearby Blenheim Palace was brand new.

WORTHING, Sussex – MONTAGUE STREET

This interesting encounter came from a lady who wrote to me from Worthing in Sussex.

In 2003, bright and early one morning, she was walking down Montague Street in Worthing, pushing her bicycle. It was already light, and she was on her way to what was then Forfar's bakers.

Ahead of her, just a few paces in front, were an old couple, probably in their 70's at least, walking along slowly arm in arm together, so that she was quite quickly catching them up. There was nothing unusual at all about them, they seemed perfectly ordinary and solid and were wearing perfectly normal clothing - nothing at all which would call any particular attention to them - except they looked quite sweet with their arms linked together like that.

She glanced down for a second, then back up.

The loving old couple had vanished. She was so close behind them, and only took her eyes off them for a split second, so there really was nowhere they could have gone and slipped out of her sight.

YORK, Yorkshire - THE THEATRE ROYAL

This incredible old theatre was founded in 1734 by Thomas Kerigan and his wife, and is well known to be haunted. The site it stands on goes back to at least Roman times, since the remains of a well have been discovered beneath its floors, and there was also a hospital on the site in the 12th Century. There is supposed to be the ghost of a Grey Lady here. She is said to be the spirit of a young nun who worked here when it was a hospital, and committed the sin of falling in love with a nobleman whom she broke her vow of chastity with. As a punishment, supposedly, she was walled up in a niche in the walls and left there to die an agonisingly slow death of thirst.

Sightings of her are apparently frequently reported, so I wrote to the Theatre and asked whether their ghosts were still active and received a very helpful reply. She has been seen many times over recent years but most of the 'supernatural' episodes (which they have assumed to be linked to the Grey Lady) have been sounds rather than sightings. My correspondent had worked there for nearly two decades, and was very sceptical about the supernatural at first. Over the years, she has changed her mind somewhat.

She said that often noises are heard; footsteps on the stone dressing rooms staircase for example, the ticking of a mantle clock in the

Greenroom and a strange dragging sound that is occasionally audible on the stage late at night. In addition shadowy figures and cold 'blasts' are seen and felt in backstage and Dressing room areas.

One occasion that she found particularly memorable was a night that she was locking up after the audience had left. She was about to leave the front of house areas and make her way to meet the Stage Door Keeper backstage when the tannoy/music relay system switched itself on and played music that wasn't even in the CD player! At first she thought crew were there and were playing tricks but as it became clear that there were only two of them in the building it quickly became apparent this was not the case.

On another occasion, some of their cleaning staff saw a woman who they took to be a new cleaner in the Dress Circle doing what they thought was sweeping. They were so convinced that there was an actual corporeal woman there that they made her a cup of tea, only to discover there was no one there at all.

Similarly, the Stage Door Keeper saw a woman, again sweeping one of the Dressing Rooms late at night, but she also disappeared very quickly.

She said that mostly the staff don't talk about the weird happenings very much or draw attention to it for fear that it will either spook or influence other people's thoughts and experiences or that they are thought barking mad!

BIBLIOGRAPHY

J. A Brooks - The Ghosts and Legends of Wales
Ivan Bunn - A return to Haunted Lowestoft
Glyndwr Edwards - Supernatural Cardiff
Keith J. Fitzpatrick-Matthews - The Cemeteries of Roman Baldock
Andrew Green - Ghosts of Today
Peter Jennings - Haunted Ipswich
Richard Jones - Haunted Castles of Britain and Ireland
Christine McCarthy - Some Ghostly Tales of Shropshire
David McGrory - Haunted Coventry
Jenny Randles - Time Storms
John and Anne Spencer - Encyclopedia of Ghosts and Spirits V2
John and Anne Spencer - Ghost Handbook
Cathy Stanworth - Shropshire Star
Peter Underwood - Guide to Ghosts and Haunted Places
John 'Willow' Williams - www.calvertonvillage.com/ghosts

www.british-history.ac.uk
Calverton Village.com
East Anglia Daily Times - Weird Suffolk
The Forces War Records
Ghostpubs.com
The Paranormal Database
Staffordshire Past Track
Strangemag.com

Other books by the Author

If you have enjoyed this book, please please leave a review wherever you bought it from. These reviews form algorithms which help other readers find the books - which is really helpful for Independent authors like myself.

I would really like it if you were to get in touch with me to tell me your own experiences of the supernatural. Without your help I have nothing to write about!

You can connect with me on Facebook or Twitter, or email me on

wa-1400@outlook.com

https://www.facebook.com/RuthRoperWylde/

https://twitter.com/RuthRoperWylde

Other books by me:

The Ghosts of Marston Vale
The Almanac of British Ghosts
The Roadmap of British Ghosts

Printed in Great Britain
by Amazon